Boat Modeling
with Dynamite Payson

Boat Modeling
with Dynamite Payson

Harold "Dynamite" Payson

International Marine Publishing
Camden, Maine

Published by International Marine Publishing

10 9 8 7 6 5 4 3 2

Copyright © 1989 International Marine Publishing, an
imprint of TAB BOOKS. TAB BOOKS is a division of McGraw-
Hill, Inc.

Library of Congress Cataloging in Publication Data

Payson, Harold H.
    Boat modeling with Dynamite Payson / Harold "Dynamite" Payson.
       p.   cm.
    Includes bibliographical references.
    ISBN 0-87742-983-9
    1. Boats and boating—Mode's. I. Title.
VM298.P39   1989
623.8'201042—dc20

                                    89-36825
                                       CIP

TAB BOOKS offers software for sale. For information and a
catalog, please contact TAB Software Department, Blue Ridge
Summit, PA 17294-0850.

Questions regarding the content of this book should be
addressed to:

International Marine Publishing
P.O. Box 220
Camden, ME 04843

Typeset by Camden Type 'n Graphics, Camden, Maine
Printed by Capital City Press, Montpelier, VT
Design by Edith Allard
Illustrated by Doug Alvord
Production by Janet Robbins
Edited by J.R. Babb, Jonathan Eaton, Tom McCarthy
Cover photos by Joe Devenny

To Amy

To Jay Hanna, from whom I learned more practical stuff in five minutes than all the boatmodeling books put together.

To Jon Wilson, for letting me use the plans for the Friendship sloop, *Amy R. Payson.*

To Peter Spectre, who got me started, then hooked, on this modeling business.

To Bob Steward, who told me I had caught "modelitis" when I told him I couldn't leave it alone.

To Dave Dillion, who lent a hand many times, and helped me really understand boat lines.

To Phil Bolger, Alan McInnis, and Captains Ken and Ellen Barnes, for the use of their plans.

To Elmer Montgomery, for his inspiration.

To Doug Alvord, whose beautiful illustrations grace these pages.

To my wife Amy, for her many hours of shared enthusiasm.

And last but definitely not least, to Jim Babb, for exemplifying what an editor is supposed to be; to Molly Mulhern and Janet Robbins, who make beautiful books; and to the rest of the IMP crew for making this a fun project.

Contents

Preface   xi
Introduction: Getting Started   xii

1   Building the Maine Lobsterboat   1
A simple, easily made toy to build your confidence.

2   12-Foot Fisherman's Skiff   9
A flat-bottomed skiff built just the same as the original.

3   The Gloucester Light Dory   27
A solid model; a fiberglass fleet; a half-model; and a planked edition.

4   Bobcat—An Instant Catboat   57
A simple method for building one curvaceous hull.

5   Cartopper   75
A featherweight, multichine beauty.

6   The Peapod   105
A strip-planked, round-bottomed classic.

7   The Friendship Sloop Amy R. Payson   147
Variations on a bread-and-butter theme.

Appendix A   Enlarging Plans   169
Appendix B   Sources   174
Glossary   175
Index   181

Even though I build full-size boats for a living, for years I've wanted to build boat models—not full-rigged ships, but down-to-earth models that matched my own levels of skill and patience. Along the way, I've been fortunate to have the successes or failures of others to inspire and shape my own ambitions. For instance, watching the expensive remains of a friend's botched kit go up in flames served as my first model-building lesson. I decided right then and there that working with stamped-out kits and balsa was not for me. Later, I learned to build boat models the easy way. Nautical architect Weston Farmer, in an article for *National Fisherman*, told of his commonsense, use-what-you-have-around-you approach to modelmaking based on paper patterns cut or traced from plans. His message—that building boat models his way was easy and fun—came through to me loud and clear, and has kept me entertained ever since.

Why build a model? George Putz, co-editor of the Mariner's Catalogs, once answered that question by saying that models are better than full-size boats:

You can build them exactly the way originals are built, in less time, with the best materials and fewer tools, at a fraction of the cost, in the comfort of your own home. And you don't have to worry about insurance, moorage, hauling and storage, maverick hurricanes, or mysterious leaks around the centerboard trunk.

You can display them on your mantelpiece, mount them on the wall, or suspend them from the ceiling with nearly invisible wires. You can even sail them around the harbor or pond if they are ballasted and rigged properly.

You can, with a straight face, tell your mother-in-law you build your models for education, recreation, historical research, or sheer, unadulterated, mindless pleasure, and she can't complain. She can't indict you for spending so much on boats that you take food from the mouths of her grandchildren.

The part about sheer unadulterated pleasure most appeals to me; it frees me to build models any way and from anything I like.

Taking a page from my own book, so to speak, I've arranged here a progression of boats, each illustrating a new scratch-building technique. We'll start with a chip-in-the-puddle version of the Maine lobsterboat that takes the least amount of work and patience but has a big payoff. Your kids will think you're a magician when you zip through this toy before their eyes in only a few minutes. Who knows, you might even kindle the boatbuilding bug in them right on the spot!

Next, to illustrate single-chine construction, elementary lofting (enlarging a boat's plans to full size), and the use of a scale rule, we'll move on to a 12-foot Maine Coast fisherman's skiff built just like the original. If you can build the model you can build the boat; Dave Dillion's plans and Doug Alvord's drawings make either a breeze.

Moving right along, we'll expand on chine construction with two versions of the famed Gloucester Light Dory—one conventionally planked, and another of solid wood that you can admire as is or use to clone fiberglass copies for the mud-puddle set. Next, we'll apply variations of Weston Farmer's modeling techniques to Phil Bolger's *Cartopper* and *Bobcat*. These are guaranteed to keep you from nodding off in your armchair.

Then we'll use a model of a fisherman's peapod to study round bottom, bent-frame construction techniques that can be applied to any round-bottom boat—full size or model, rowboat or clipper ship.

Last, but far from least, we'll explore a new wrinkle on the lift method of modelbuilding—a quick and easy way to build accurate and elegant models of decked-over boats, such as Friendship sloops and sardine carriers.

For many, building the models will be an end in itself. But to some, the models will be a jumping-off point, a way to ease into full-size boatbuilding with a minimum of expense. So I'll reemphasize this: Most of these models are built the same way and, in many instances, from the same materials as the full-size boats. If you think of this as a modelbuilder's book *and* a boat-builder's bootcamp, you'll be right on the mark.

Building all these models was fun, and I learned something in the process: be adaptable, and make do with what you have. That's what this book is all about.

Getting Started

Since it is unlikely that museums will be after your first boat model—or mine either, for that matter—you're free to build any way you like. I'm not advocating sloppy workmanship or using inferior materials; just don't burden yourself with someone else's standards that may be far beyond your capabilities at this early stage in your modeling career. That's why this progressive family of boats starts with the Maine lobsterboat—a kid's puddle boat made from 2 x 4 ends. If you goof it up, throw it in the stove.

But before we get started, a word of warning: Whether you're building a model or a full-size boat, this boatbuilding business can be addictive. It's hard to know when to stop. I've often spent hours wrestling with a real or imagined obstacle before dropping it in disgust, getting away from it for a while, and later having the answer come popping out of the clear blue. For me it works best to think about the problem just before going to sleep; in the morning, there's my answer.

So keep at it. Eventually a day will come when you see at a glance what your untrained eye once took hours to see, or never saw at all. This is something that you will realize yourself, without anyone telling you, and it comes only from repetition.

While I'm at it, here's another warning for you: If you're married and your partner isn't the least bit interested in what you're doing, drop the project once in a while. Maybe you'll be spared the experience of one newly married boatbuilder of my acquaintance, whose young wife appeared late one night in his workshop shouting, "If I looked more like a boat you might spend some time with *me!*"

Wood

Ribbon-cut cedar knotted without steam (top); and maple frame tied after soaking in ammonia.

I get lots of calls from prospective boatbuilders all over the country asking if their native woods are suitable for building boats. Chances are some of it is, if they know what to pick. I've seen boats planked with beautiful, straight-grained cypress,

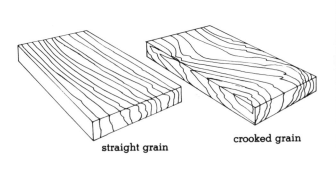

straight grain

crooked grain

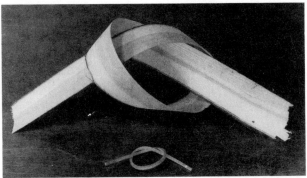

and I have a piece of the same wood that's fit only for a doorstop. It isn't so much the species that matters, but the quality of the particular piece of wood. Look at whatever species is common in your area, but keep these properties in mind: the wood should bend nicely, without being brittle; it should be easy to shape, which usually means a softwood; and it should be *straight grained.*

Here in Maine I'm sold on our native white cedar; even without steaming you can tie a knot in it. I get mine from a local furniture factory, much of it from its scrap pile. Yes, it's free, but I wouldn't mind paying for it to get what I want. And speaking of furniture, take a hard look at that maple, cherry, or birch table headed for the dump. Therein could lie the perfect wood for the timbers and backbone of any number of models, including the peapod in this book.

For untalented scroungers, or urban dwellers who may find lumberyards few and far between, hobby shops can supply 1/64- through 1/4-inch basswood or birch plywood, in 1-foot by 2- or 4-foot sheets, for prices ranging, at this writing, from $2.00 to $8.00. With its uniform length, width, and milled-to-a-cat's-whisker thickness, a few sheets of this saves a lot of time. But the monotonous grain turns me off, and I use little of it.

Picking the right wood for the job at hand is a highly personal choice. Pick what you like to work with, and go for it. What about soft and ugly balsa? *Bahh!*

Power Tools

I was asked recently, "If you were just starting to set up shop, what power tool would you get first?" I shot right back, "A *table saw!*" This is the foundation of the whole family of tools. You can make a gutter for your house or saw out precision parts for your model; you can rough out large pieces that will later be shaped with other tools. Start with a table saw and you can produce about anything.

More to the point, a table saw will free you from depending on a hobby shop for precut, accurately dimensioned wood. My 8-inch table saw makes child's play of sawing 1/32- or 1/16-inch planking for models. A 10-inch saw, with its greater depth of cut to handle wider planking stock, works even better. Using a hollow-ground planer blade (a combination rip and cut-off blade, with teeth in line rather than askew), with its narrow kerf and extremely smooth cut, I can pile up a bunch of perfect planks in no time at all, and never go near a hobby shop.

"That's nice," you say, "but what can I do with a pile of skinny planks? Boats come in all sizes and shapes." Nothing to it. To get the width you want, just lay a piece of waxed paper down on a smooth surface—your table saw, a Formica table, whatever—and edge-glue together as many planks as it takes, arranging them into attractive grain patterns. Don't just put a

Sawing out plank stock. If your saw won't cut as deep as you want, just make two passes, like this.

bead of glue on the joints; make a wooden paddle and slather it right on, like mustard on a hot dog. If the planks don't want to lie flat, cover them with waxed paper and weight them down. When the glue is dry, sand them with 220-grit sandpaper to get rid of excess glue. Compared with relying on the hobby shop's bland-looking (and expensive) plywood, freedom of choice like this is worth a little extra work.

Once your table saw is set up for a job, saw out all the wood of a given thickness you need (you can estimate this fairly well by looking at the plans). Few things are more irritating than finding out you didn't saw out enough planking, sawing out another batch, and finding out you're just a little off.

A *bandsaw* is a great tool for sawing larger pieces of wood, such as the solid dory model. Opened fully, my 10-inch bandsaw just barely made the cut. A 12- or 14-inch saw would have worked better, and the larger saw tends to break fewer blades. (For best cutting, buy only hardened, skip-tooth blades.) But use what you have; it isn't necessary to have the best or latest tools. I bought both the table saw and the bandsaw in my less affluent days, and have never found it necessary to upgrade.

A *scroll saw* completes the power inventory. This works great for cutting smaller parts in wood or metal where fineness of cut matters. All three of my power saws are Delta, and have served me well over the years. Though both the table and bandsaw are a little small for some jobs, they are OK when kept at peak performance—and that means *sharp!* If you'd rather do this yourself than pay a saw sharpener, see my book: *Keeping the Cutting Edge: Setting and Sharpening Hand and Power Saws (WoodenBoat* Publications, 1983).

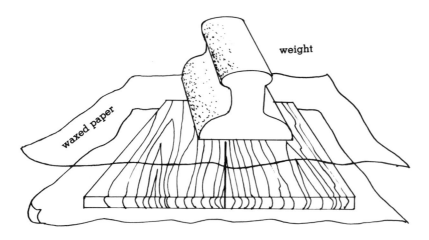

weight

waxed paper

Edge-gluing stock.

You may have some of these on hand. If you have to go out and buy the whole kit at one whack, figure on $100 to $150, depending on your shopping abilities. You'll need:

Hand Tools

- magnifying glass, for reading plans
- architect's rule—indispensable
- A 2-ounce jeweler's ball peen hammer. This is great for heading over brass wire or driving small pins.
- miniature machinist's vise
- miniature hand drill
- set of micro drill bits, from #54 through #80
- farrier's (horseshoer's) rasp
- set of Swiss-pattern, tool-and-die-maker's files: the 12 standard needle shapes
- jeweler's saw, for fine cuts in any material
- razor saw and replaceable blades
- micro plane, for delicate planing jobs
- extra-fine needlenose pliers
- diagonal cutting pliers
- bellows-type glue applicator
- $1/32$-inch sheet brass: one strip, 4 by 10 inches
- sandpaper: 100, 220, 320 grit
- package of emery boards
- roll of sticky-back tape
- pincurlers (yes, pincurlers)
- $1/2$- and $3/4$-inch brass dressmaker's pins

In some circumstances you can use ordinary common pins, but I usually find them to be too large for delicate work. In addition, the small brass pins can be cut, sanded down, and, because they don't rust, left in your work forever: a big time-saver.

Brass dressmaker's pins can be purchased by the pound from Newark Dressmaker Supply (see Appendix B for ad-

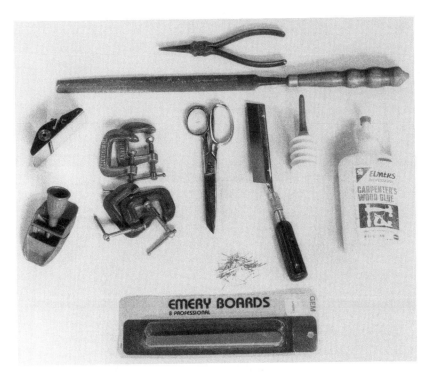

The basic tool kit. You'll need this for every model in this book.

dresses). A pound will probably last you a lifetime. You can purchase a tiny bubble pack of 100 pins in most sewing shops for about 60¢, but I drop or bend a lot of them, so for me it's by the pound. But by the pound or the piece, I for sure wouldn't want to tackle modelmaking without them.

Glues

Vast arrays of epoxies, superglues, fillers, and coatings—most anything you can imagine—are readily available, but for most projects I get by nicely with Franklin Titebond. It's a quick-grabbing glue, and joints need only be held together for a few minutes—even in your hands. It isn't waterproof, however. If soaked for a few days your model will come apart, but for mantelpiece projects it's perfect. Elmer's White Glue works well, too, although it's slower to grab. This is a feature you may want to bear in mind if you have a long seam to fiddle with.

Finishing Materials

Although I expect it's different in the big cities, around here I've found that mail-order suppliers offer the best selection. The best one I've found is Micro-Mark (see Appendix B), a specialist in small hand and power tools, along with everything else you would want to get started in the modelmaking business. Except for the dressmaker's pins and the pincurlers, their catalog contains everything I've mentioned, including their impressive "miniature lumberyard": 4- by 24-inch sheets of basswood, walnut, mahogany, and cherry, $1/32$ inch through 2 inches thick. They also carry top-quality, aircraft-grade birch plywood in 6- by 12-inch or 12- by 24-inch sheets, 1/64 through 1/4 inch thick.

Micro-Mark also offers 94 different colors—enough to suit almost everyone, I'd think—of Floquil's scale model paints, which, because they have pigments ground to scale size, don't obscure fine detail. If you decide to go that route, plan to buy their thinner, retarders, and all the rest too. If you find fault with their paint, and you've thinned it with kerosene, you won't have a leg to stand on. Their thinners could be plain old mineral spirits for all I know, but don't chance it just to save a buck.

All these colors are nice, but that stuff is a bit sophisticated for my tastes, so I'll just stick with what I can stir up at home myself, and think about using pretty colors later. After spending all that time selecting wood grain, why cover it up with paint? I like to use varnish thinned down 30 to 40 percent with turpentine, and add a dollop of Japan dryer to help it set up. Thinning varnish is the secret to a good varnishing job. My work, the varnish dipped right from the can, used to look as if someone dumped a load of gravel on it, but no more. Using thinned varnish, most everyone can get a professional-looking satin finish.

Measurement

Most of the plans in this book, and virtually all full-size boat plans, use a form of shorthand to express dimensions in feet, inches, and eighths of an inch. If you see 3-8-6, think 3 feet, 8 inches, and 6/8 (or 3/4) inch. Contrast that with writing 3' 83/4", then trying to read it through sawdust, glue, and coffee stains. If a plus sign follows the eighth, add 1/16 inch. For example, 9-8-5+ is read as 9 feet 8 and 11/16 inches (5/8 inch plus 1/16 inch).

Although it looks confusing, it is the essence of simplicity, and effectively prevents errors from creeping into the work of even the densest among us.

To round out your supplies you'll want a good-quality paint brush, about 1/2- or 5/8-inch at the ferrule, and 1 inch or so at the business end. Err on the side of a little larger rather than smaller. It's a mistake to paint a model by hand using a small brush. The job goes so slowly that the paint dries between strokes, ensuring a poor paint job.

The Plans

Now that we're armed with tools and materials it's time to have a look at the plans. There are several ways of approaching this simple style of modelmaking; you are welcome to adopt any method you prefer.

By far the quickest, easiest, and most accurate way to build models—and my favorite—is to get the full-scale plans, cut them up, and use them for templates. What could be easier and more accurate than cutting full-size patterns directly from the designer's drawings. But because most of the models in this book are built from plans drawn originally for full-size boats, and a nautical architect counts on these for his sole source of income, this is not necessarily the cheapest way to go. But if you figure how long it will take to draw these plans full size (a couple of hours with a little practice), and how much your time is worth to you, you may find this method less expensive than you think. Besides, you may decide that after building the model, you're ready for the full-size boat. (Ordering information for the plans in this book is in Appendix B.)

If you want to keep your plans intact, or you're not feeling particularly flush; if you want to learn how real boats are lofted, or you have lots of time on your hands, you can simply measure the boat's parts directly from the plans and transfer their shapes to wood. This means using scale rules, battens, pins, and a lot of time, but if you're looking at 10 feet of snow out your window, why not? (For a complete discussion of this method, see Appendix A.)

If you're strapped both for time and cash, there's yet another way. If you have access to a big photocopying machine, you can have the plans blown up or down—any way you want, although I prefer bigger; it's easier to build. These plans can be glued directly to wood, or the lines can be transferred by brushing the copy with acetone and pressing it against the wood. A quick price check here in midcoast, small-town Maine found prices ranging from $4.80 to $6.00 per sheet to enlarge the plans in this book to a full 24 by 36 inches. This method is not without its problems, however. Lens distortion, page curvature, and line thickness make this method somewhat less accurate than the other methods.

There are also many plans out there (I know, I've sent out my share of them) that have served their purpose— enabling their owners to build full-size boats—but are still intact, crying out for another use. How about a model for the mantel? Then there are other plans out there that were never used at all. With plans spread out, some would-be builders get cold feet and don't want to gamble their skills against the cost of materials for a full-size boat. If you're one of these, come along with me, at minimum risk, for an adventure in modelmaking.

Building the Maine Lobsterboat

I owe the inspiration for this lovely little toy to the late Axel Gronros, boatbuilder and owner of Rockland Boat Shop, in Rockland, Maine. I used to drop by his Sea Street shop for pot warp or other fishing supplies on trips into town from Metinic Island, where I was lobstering back during the late Forties and early Fifties. The dirt-floored retail store was connected to the boatshop by a brick walk, which for me was like following the yellow brick road to the land of Oz.

I visited there one day with my son, David, who was then just a baby in his mother's arms. When Axel spied David, he stopped what he was doing, selected a scrap piece of wood from the ample pile around his big bandsaw, and sawed out a boat for him right on the spot—passing it straight into the reaching arms of this bulging-eyed kid hollering "BOAT!"

Years later, when I could afford my own bandsaw, I still remembered how Axel produced such a nice shape so quickly. He tilted his bandsaw to 15 or so degrees and, from an ordinary flat board, and without changing the saw table's angle, produced it in one cut, giving it a raked stem, flared sides, and even a curved and raked transom: all the goodies that make a boat pretty.

Materials Needed:

- a foot-and-a-half chunk of 2 x 4
- waterproof glue
- twine
- paint
- kid
- mudpuddle

Tools Needed:

- bandsaw or sabersaw
- handsaw
- wide, flat chisel
- vise
- spokeshave
- sandpaper

Let's Build a Boat

When I built my own version, I did it much the same way as Axel, only I got a little fancier: I gave the boat a typical lobster-boat sheer and tacked a deckhouse on it. It added a lot to the boat's looks, and it was easy to do.

Cut out the sheer profile from the plans, trace them from the book, or photocopy them—whichever way you've decided to go—and lay out the sheer profile on both edges of a foot-long chunk of 2 x 4.

Using a hardened 3/8- or 1/2-inch skip-tooth blade (a 1/4-inch blade will give you a wavering cut), set your bandsaw table flat (0 degrees) and saw along the sheer, then finish the new deck with a spokeshave and sandpaper.

Now, lay the deck plan on the deck and trace around it. Set your bandsaw to 15 degrees, and, with the bow facing away from you, start the cut on the port bow. Saw toward the port stern quarter, turning the boat clockwise as you go; saw

Clockwise from upper left: Trace the sheer profile on your wood....Saw out the sheer profile....Smooth the deck.... Trace the deck plan.

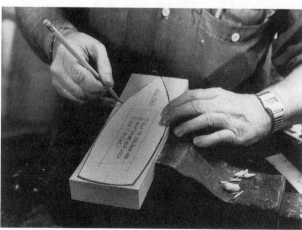

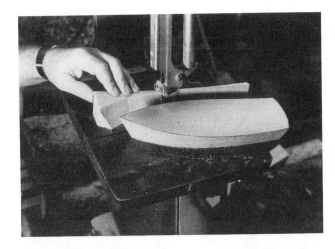

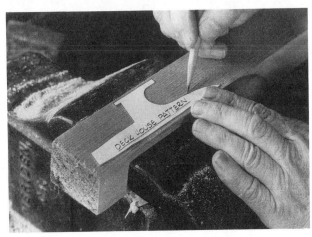

around the stern, and back up the starboard side to the bow. Save the scraps from the sides, and either tack them to a piece of wood to make a cradle, or tack them to the boat itself; either way will make working on the boat easier and prevent the vise jaws from damaging the hull.

The bandsaw is really the best tool for this work, but not everyone has one. If you don't, you can cut out the body plan OK with a sabersaw, but most sabersaws won't cut deep enough to handle the sheer profile. Not to worry! Use a handsaw to make a series of cuts down to the sheer line, about ½ inch apart and right across the hull; chisel out the waste; and smooth her up with a spokeshave. This simple trick gets rid of excess wood fast and safely. Just don't skimp on the saw cuts; keep them close together, and stop about ⅛ inch shy of the mark. I can tell you from experience those teeth cut deeper than you think.

A bowsaw—something like a heavy-duty coping saw—could replace a bandsaw as well, but if you don't have a bandsaw, I'll bet you don't have a bowsaw either. I've never owned one.

Clockwise from upper left: Tilt the saw and saw out the body (save the scraps)....No bandsaw? Cut parallel saw kerfs to the sheer line ...and chisel away the waste....Trace the deckhouse pattern.

① START WITH A PIECE OF 2x4, 2x6 OR 2x8 11" LONG OF FAIRLY CLEAR SPRUCE.

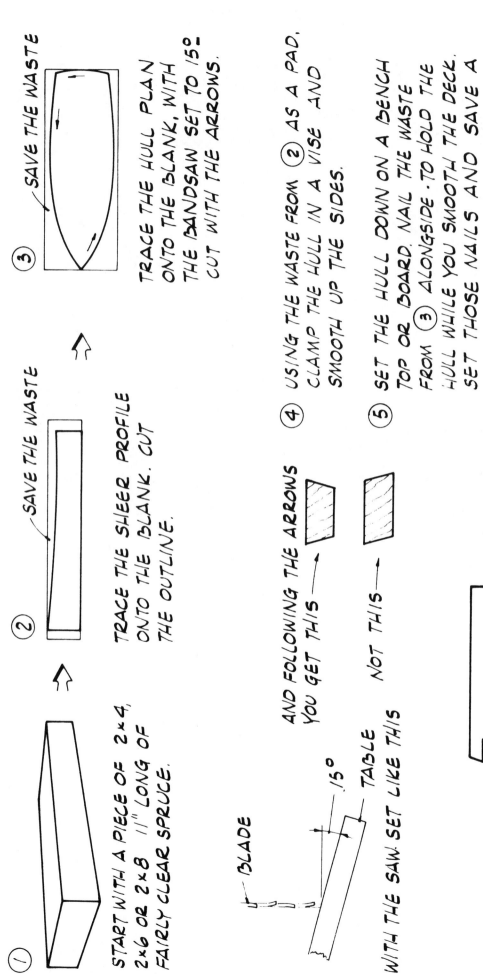

BLADE

15°

TABLE

WITH THE SAW SET LIKE THIS

AND FOLLOWING THE ARROWS YOU GET THIS →

NOT THIS →

② SAVE THE WASTE

TRACE THE SHEER PROFILE ONTO THE BLANK. CUT THE OUTLINE.

③ SAVE THE WASTE

TRACE THE HULL PLAN ONTO THE BLANK, WITH THE BANDSAW SET TO 15° CUT WITH THE ARROWS.

④ USING THE WASTE FROM ② AS A PAD, CLAMP THE HULL IN A VISE AND SMOOTH UP THE SIDES.

⑤ SET THE HULL DOWN ON A BENCH TOP OR BOARD. NAIL THE WASTE FROM ③ ALONGSIDE · TO HOLD THE HULL WHILE YOU SMOOTH THE DECK. SET THOSE NAILS AND SAVE A BLADE.

⑥ TRACE THE DECKHOUSE PATTERN ONTO A PIECE OF 2x4 · CUT OUT AND SMOOTH UP. DYNAMITE SAYS THOSE CURVES CAN BE CUT WITH A 1/4" BLADE.

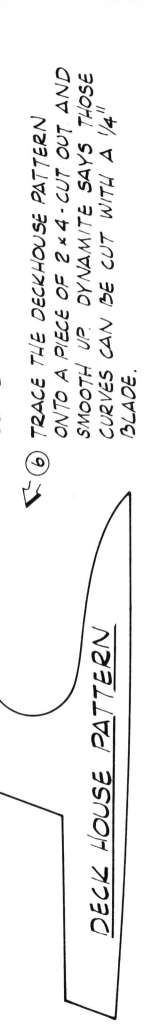

DECK HOUSE PATTERN

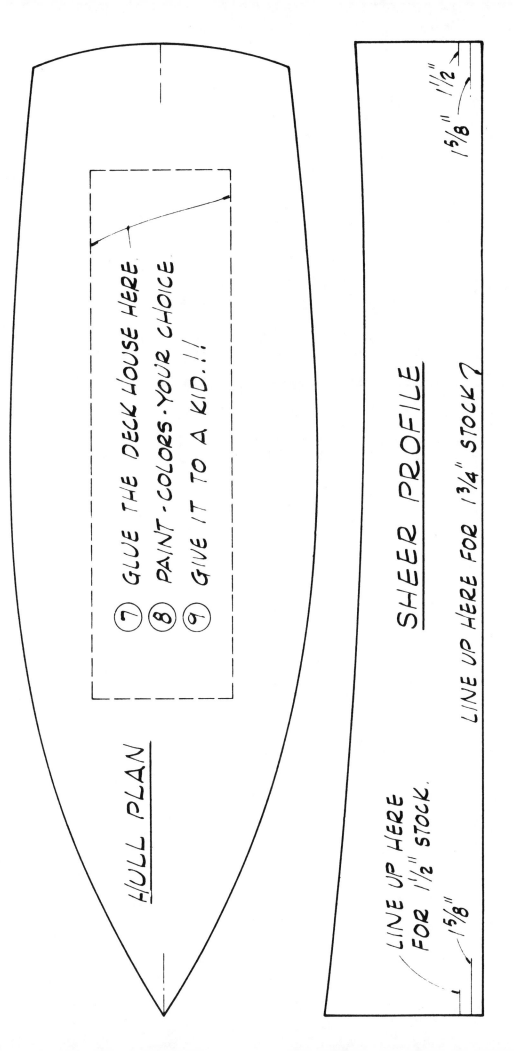

HULL PLAN

⑦ GLUE THE DECK HOUSE HERE.
⑧ PAINT - COLORS - YOUR CHOICE.
⑨ GIVE IT TO A KID.!!

SHEER PROFILE

LINE UP HERE FOR 1¾" STOCK↗

LINE UP HERE
FOR 1½" STOCK.
↙1⅝"

↗1½"
1⅝"↙

THE MAINE LOBSTER BOAT.

The plans for this lobsterboat are full
size. Trace or photocopy them 1:1, right
from the book.

All the cuts for the deckhouse can be made with a coping saw, or with the same bandsaw blade you used for the hull, except for the after part of the canopy. This has a quicker turn, and will need a ¼-inch blade to follow it.

Cut out the deckhouse, smooth it up, glue it on with any waterproof glue, such as Weldwood; paint it your choice of colors, paint on her name and home port and she's done. Add a puddle and a piece of string on a stick, and you've made a kid some happy.

Now all you need is a kid.

2

12-Foot Fisherman's Skiff

If you gather by now that I spent a lot of time hanging around Rockland Boat Shop you're right. Not that I didn't hang around any others I could find—but Rockland Boat Shop always had the most going on. There were usually three or four carvel-planked lobsterboats a-building at once, and the sound of ringing hammers was music to my ears. It was also the first place a real boatbuilder like Axel Gronros ever gave me the time of day—some of his workmen even answered my questions—and I ate it all up.

In the winter, to fill in slack time between building bigger boats, the shop crew built a 12-foot fisherman's skiff, which used up the narrow ends of leftover planks; nothing was wasted in a Maine boatshop back during the depression. The skiffs were built upside down on a jig (a temporary building frame that defines the boat's shape), set up to a comfortable working height that enabled the workers to build them all day long, one after the other. That seemed smart to me. If you build your boat upside down, gravity works for rather than against you; flared sides lie in against the jig instead of falling off; when you put the bottom on you pound nails down instead of up—pretty neat. The jig even had thumb cleats to hold the precut sides precisely in place. If you wanted the skiff to

Materials Needed:

- about 3 running feet of straight-grained 2 x 4 or equivalent
- wood glue
- 60-, 80-, and 220-grit sandpaper
- varnish
- turpentine
- Japan dryer

Tools Needed:

- table saw with a sharp planer blade
- razor saw
- scale rule
- bevel gauge
- miniature hand plane
- dividers
- several micro clamps
- 5/8" paintbrush

be slightly wider or narrower at either end you just shoved the boat ahead or back on the jig a little. Not bad, I thought, not bad at all!

Axel finally allowed me to copy the jig for his 12-foot skiff. In fact, took it right home with me I did, along with the patterns for the sides, transom, stem—the whole works.

I wasn't long in bringing my first skiff up for Axel to inspect; I didn't want him to think he had spent his time with me in vain. When I first pulled into the yard with it he said nothing, but he knew where to look. He went to the stern and looked down in, then walked to the bow and took another look. He didn't speak English very well, and was consequently a man of few words, but when he finally swung his eyes from the boat and looked at me with a big smile, I knew he was pleased. The end fit of the chines was "humming tight"—no half-inch of putty here. When we make the model, I'll show you how to make these joints. Other than the toy lobsterboat, this is the easiest boat in the fleet to build. It's built just like the full-size original, and it's all sawed out with your table saw.

Getting Started

The Jig

The jig gives the boat its shape, so let's look at that first. You can make it as shown in the plans, from stock sawed 1/8 inch by 5/16 or 3/8 inch (you'll need about 8 running feet), or you can use solid stuff—most anything from aircraft plywood to cardboard. If you plan to keep it around to show your friends, the first method looks neatest; if speed of accomplishment is your thing, go the solid-jig route.

Place a sharp planer blade in your table saw and, at one setting of the saw (this keeps all the stock the same thickness), cut all the wood you need. Pay close attention to the wood's grain before you start cutting. To get nice-looking, close-grained stock, as well as more stable wood, saw across the grain instead of parallel to it. Saw the strips in 2- to 3-foot lengths, using a push-stick to shove the end along while pulling slightly on the end away from you; cut them to shorter lengths later by hand. Cutting long lengths keeps your fingers away from the saw blade, an important safety feature.

I'll stick my neck out right now and say I don't use a safety guard that rides up as I push my work through my table saw. I want to see exactly where the saw is when I'm using it and the guard hides what I'm doing. They say don't do it, but that's my

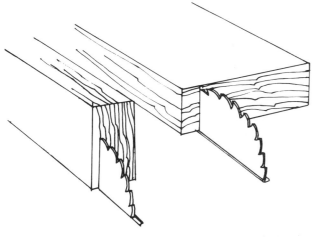

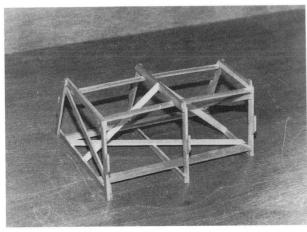

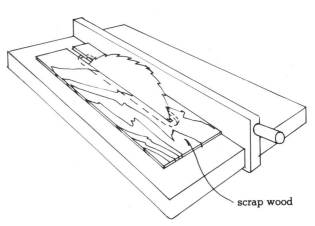

scrap wood

way; you do it your own way—whichever seems to be the least risk to your fingers.

After you get out your jig stock, lay a piece of waxed paper or plastic wrap over the full-size drawings, tracings, plans, or photocopies of all three jig station molds, taping the paper (or wrap) in place. Keep your rule in your pocket and just lay those sticks you've cut right on the drawing, building the molds right there. (Don't forget the thumb cleats.) This is as accurate as you can get. Mark the centerline on each mold, all around; space them apart as shown in profile on Sheet 2-2, and brace the jig off.

These plans are drawn for building either the full-size skiff or the model. The butt joints shown on the plans for the bottom and side panels are for the full-size plywood version, built from 4 x 8 sheets. For the model, ignore the butt joints.

Using 1/16-inch stock, saw two pieces for the sides a minimum width of 2¼ inches by about 19 inches long. Cut out the side pattern from the plans with scissors and lay it on your

Clockwise from upper left: Saw across the grain, not parallel to it....When sawing thin strips, run a wider board through the saw first to close up the blade's slot, then saw out the strips. Yes, I know I'm not using a blade guard. I want to see what I'm doing. But I am using a push stick. I suggest you do, too—blade guard or not....The finished jig.

Getting Out the Parts

wood, keeping in mind that the top edge of the panel is dead straight and the bottom part is curved. Mark the seat locations and the point on the plans marked 2-foot 9¾-inches (Sheet 2-3) that locates the side panels' fore and aft position on the jig at station 3.

The seats and the transom can be gotten out of a piece of wood sawn 3/32 inch by 2 inches by about 21 inches. Cut out the transom, then bevel its sides 15 degrees. The chines are 3/32 by 3/16 inch, also beveled 15 degrees, but on both edges. Why both? So the top of the chine sheds water; they'll also bend in easier. The two clamps are 1/16 by 5/32 inch, square-edged. The three drag strips are 3/32 by 5/32 inch; seat frames and risers, 3/32 by 5/32 inch, and the transom frame, 5/32 by 5/32 inch beveled 15 degrees (sides and bottom). Make the transom side frames an inch or so longer than the transom sides.

If all these figures for the boat's components seem over-powering, remember: They are not carved in stone. Seats, seat risers, gunwales, planking—all can be varied a little to suit. Accuracy in cutting *is* needed, however, with the main pieces: the sides, transom, and stem. The materials list calls for the model's stem to be ¼ by ¼ inch by about 3 inches. The plans give the stem's dimensions for the full-size boat: molded 1¾ inches (the profile view) and sided 1⅞ inches (the transverse width). For safety's sake, and for easy sawing, cut the stem from a piece of wood you can hang on to—a piece perhaps a couple inches wide by a foot or so long. Using the 1½ inches-to-the-foot scale on your rule, measure a scrap of wood to cut to a scale 1⅞ inches (15/64—¼ inch is near enough for most of us) thick. Run the scrap through the saw and measure it again to make sure you are right on the money. Draw a centerline on what will become the face of the stem; set your table saw to 29 degrees, and saw the bevel both sides.

Years of wobbling saw blades have a way of widening table saw insert slots—an accident waiting to happen if it starts to eat a small piece of wood and you grab for it. To avoid this danger, before you make those bevel cuts (or straight cuts either for that matter), run a scrap piece of wood into the saw blade until it covers the slot and the table side where you will be sawing. To prevent kickback, clamp it in place. Set your saw blade so that it just shows through the wood you are going to saw—definitely another safety feature for the fingers—and saw out the stem.

This is a good place to decide how you'll plank the bottom. If you are in a hurry, you can plank the bottom in one crack with a sheet of aircraft plywood; if you're not, you can cross-plank it in the time-honored way using various widths of planking. I cross-planked mine with wood I sawed out myself in the widths you see on the plans: 3/8 inch and 1/2 inch (on the real boat, 3 inches and 4 inches) by about 3/32 inch thick. Alternate the planking widths as shown; this was the way it was done on the full-size boat. Again, there is room for flexibility here; 5-inch widths work OK too, but I wouldn't go any wider.

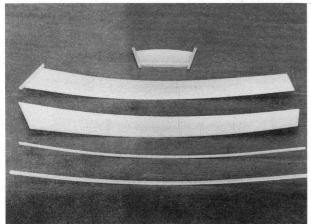

Clockwise from upper left: Marking the side panels.... Sawing out the stem. Cut it to size *after* you've cut the bevel.... Side panels, chines, and transom, ready to go on the jig. The stem and the transom framing have been glued in place.

Sheet 2-1
Enlarge 220 percent for full-size plans.

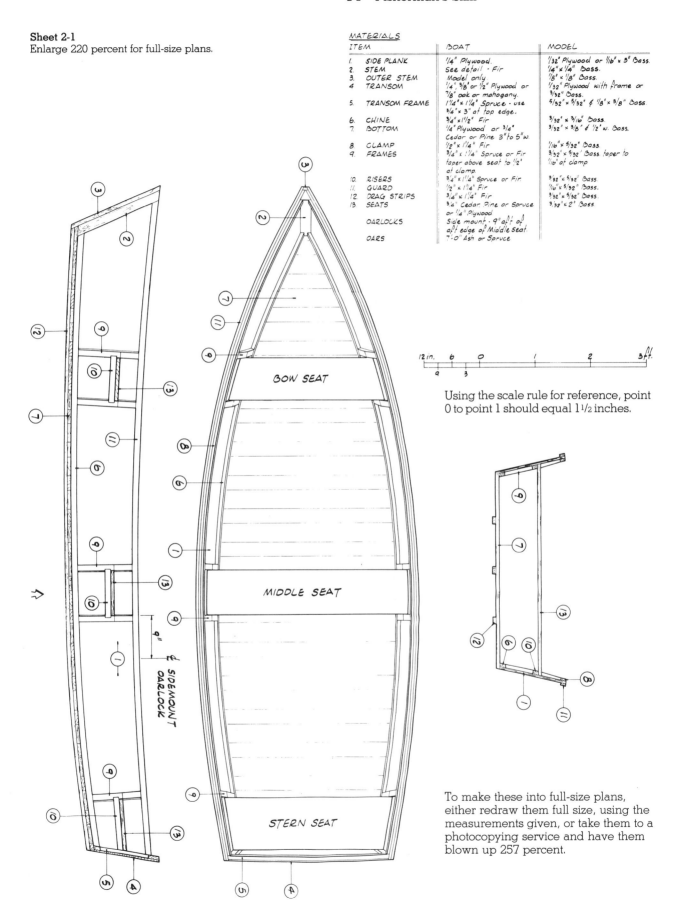

MATERIALS

ITEM		BOAT	MODEL
1.	SIDE PLANK	1/4" Plywood.	1/32" Plywood or 1/16" x 3" Bass.
2.	STEM	See detail - Fir	1/4" x 1/4" Bass.
3.	OUTER STEM	Model only	1/8" x 1/8" Bass.
4.	TRANSOM	1/4", 3/8" or 1/2" Plywood or 7/8" oak or mahogany.	1/32" Plywood with frame or 3/32" Bass.
5.	TRANSOM FRAME	1 1/4" x 1 1/4" Spruce - use 3/4" x 3" at top edge.	5/32" x 5/32" & 1/8" x 3/8" Bass.
6.	CHINE	3/4" x 1 1/2" Fir	3/32" x 3/16" Bass.
7.	BOTTOM	1/4" Plywood or 3/4" Cedar or Pine 3" to 5" w.	3/32" x 3/8" & 1/2" w. Bass.
8.	CLAMP	1/2" x 1 1/4" Fir	1/16" x 3/32" Bass.
9.	FRAMES	3/4" x 1 1/4" Spruce or Fir taper above seat to 1/2" at clamp.	3/32" x 5/32" Bass. taper to 1/16" at clamp
10.	RISERS	3/4" x 1 1/4" Spruce. or Fir.	3/32" x 5/32" Bass.
11.	GUARD	1/2" x 1 1/4" Fir	1/16" x 5/32" Bass.
12.	DRAG STRIPS	3/4" x 1 1/4" Fir	3/32" x 5/32" Bass.
13.	SEATS	3/4" Cedar, Pine or Spruce or 1/4" Plywood	3/32" x 2" Bass.
	OARLOCKS	Side mount - 9" aft of aft edge of Middle Seat.	
	OARS	7'-0" Ash or Spruce	

BOW SEAT

MIDDLE SEAT

9"

℄ SIDEMOUNT OARLOCK

STERN SEAT

12 in.   6   0   1   2   3 ft.
     9   3

Using the scale rule for reference, point 0 to point 1 should equal 1 1/2 inches.

To make these into full-size plans, either redraw them full size, using the measurements given, or take them to a photocopying service and have them blown up 257 percent.

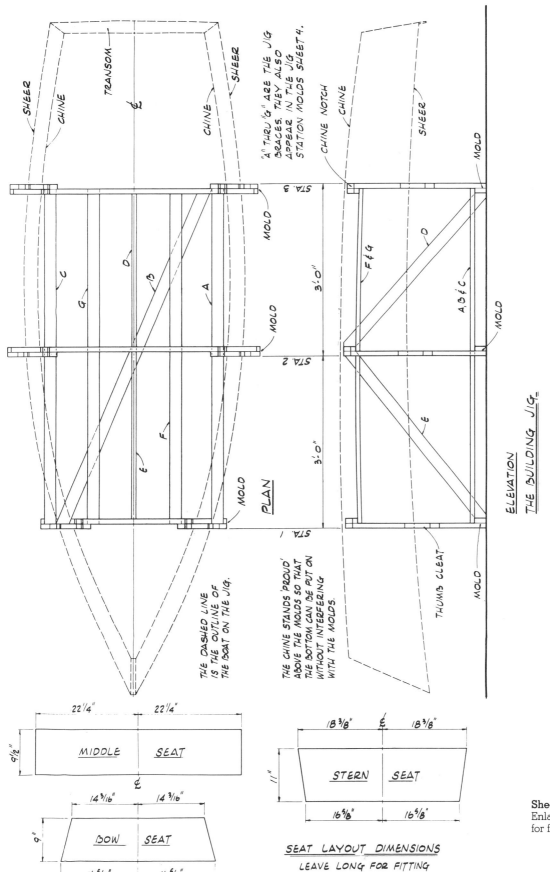

"A" THRU "G" ARE THE JIG BRACES. THEY ALSO APPEAR IN THE JIG STATION MOLDS SHEET 4.

SHEER

CHINE

TRANSOM

℄

CHINE

SHEER

MOLD

STA. 3

MOLD

3'-0"

MOLD

STA. 2

3'-0"

MOLD

STA. 1

PLAN

THE DASHED LINE IS THE OUTLINE OF THE BOAT ON THE JIG.

THE CHINE STANDS 'PROUD' ABOVE THE MOLDS SO THAT THE BOTTOM CAN BE PUT ON WITHOUT INTERFERING WITH THE MOLDS.

CHINE NOTCH

CHINE

SHEER

MOLD

F & G

D

A, B & C

MOLD

E

MOLD

THUMB CLEAT

ELEVATION

THE BUILDING JIG

22 1/4"   22 1/4"

9 1/2"

MIDDLE   SEAT

℄

14 3/16"   14 3/16"

9"

BOW   SEAT

16 5/8"   16 5/8"

18 3/8"   ℄   18 3/8"

11"

STERN   SEAT

16 5/8"   16 5/8"

SEAT LAYOUT DIMENSIONS
LEAVE LONG FOR FITTING

Sheet 2-2
Enlarge 257 percent
for full-size plans.

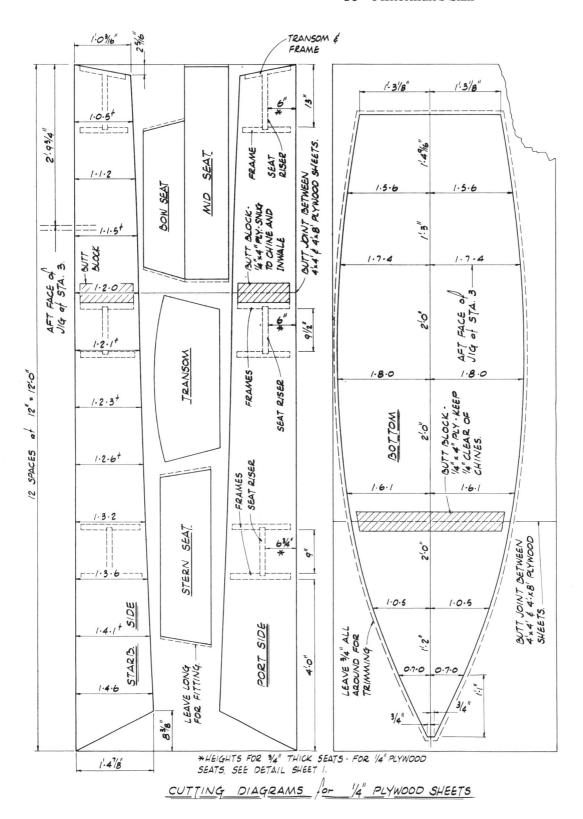

TRANSOM & FRAME

1'-0 3/16" 2 5/16"

BOW SEAT

MID SEAT

1'-0·5†

2'-9 3/4"

1'-1·2

1'-1·5†

AFT FACE of JIG of STA. 3

BUTT BLOCK

1'-2·0

1'-2·1†

TRANSOM

1'-2·3†

1'-2·6†

1'-3·2

1'-3·6

STERN SEAT.

1'-4·1†

STARB'D SIDE

1'-4·6

12 SPACES at 12" = 12'-0"

8 3/8"

1'-4 7/8"

LEAVE LONG FOR FITTING.

FRAME

SEAT RISER

* 6"

1'-3"

BUTT BLOCK. 1/4"x4" PLY. SNUG TO CHINE AND INWALE

BUTT JOINT BETWEEN 4'x4' & 4'x8' PLYWOOD SHEETS.

FRAMES

SEAT RISER

*6"

9 1/2"

FRAMES

SEAT RISER

PORT SIDE

6 3/4"

9"

4'-0"

*HEIGHTS FOR 3/4" THICK SEATS. FOR 1/4" PLYWOOD SEATS, SEE DETAIL SHEET I.

1'-3 1/8" 1'-3 1/8"

1'-4 9/16"

1'-5·6 1'-5·6

1'-3"

1'-7·4 1'-7·4

AFT FACE of JIG of STA. 3

2'-0"

1'-8·0 1'-8·0

BOTTOM

2'-0"

BUTT BLOCK. 1/4"x4" PLY. KEEP 1/4" CLEAR OF CHINES.

1'-6·1 1'-6·1

2'-0"

BUTT JOINT BETWEEN 4'x4' & 4'x8' PLYWOOD SHEETS.

1'-0·5 1'-0·5

LEAVE 3/4" ALL AROUND FOR TRIMMING

1'-2"

0·7·0 0·7·0

1·1"

3/4" 3/4"

CUTTING DIAGRAMS for 1/4" PLYWOOD SHEETS

Sheet 2-3
Enlarge 257 percent for full-size plans.

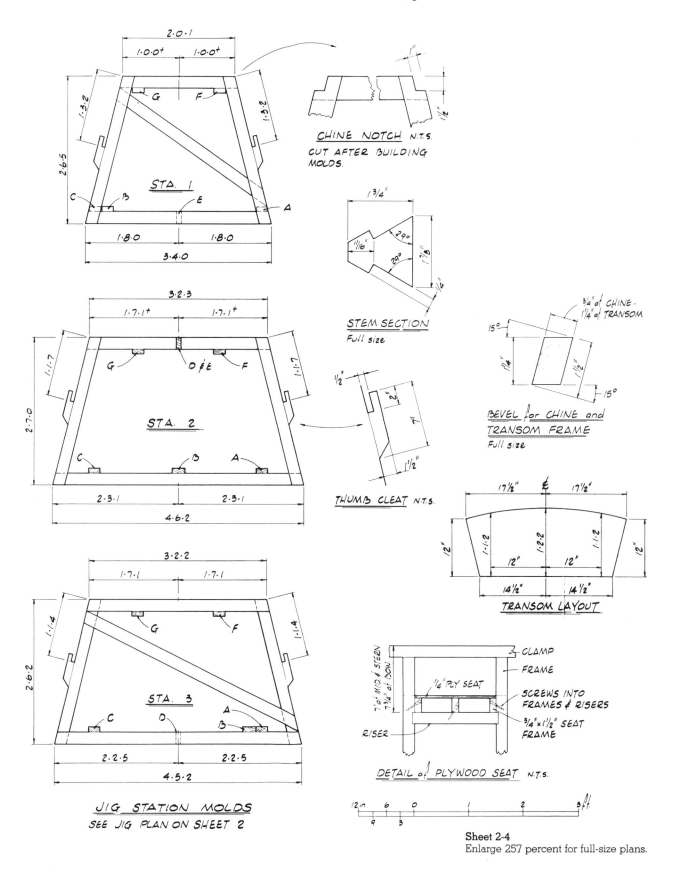

2·0·1

1·0·0+   1·0·0+

1·5·2   1·5·2

G   F

2·6·5

STA. 1

C   B   E   A

1·8·0   1·8·0

3·4·0

CHINE NOTCH N.T.S.
CUT AFTER BUILDING
MOLDS.

1 3/4"

29°
11/16"   1 7/8"
29°
1/2"

STEM SECTION
Full size

3·2·3

1·7·1+   1·7·1+

1·1·7   1·1·7

G   D & E   F

2·7·0

STA. 2

C   B   A

2·3·1   2·3·1

4·6·2

3/4" at CHINE
1 1/4" at TRANSOM

15°
1 1/4"   1 1/2"
15°

BEVEL for CHINE and
TRANSOM FRAME
Full size

1/2"
2"
7"
1 1/2"

THUMB CLEAT N.T.S.

17 1/2"   ₵   17 1/2"

12"   1·1·2   1·2·2   1·1·2   12"

12"   12"

14 1/2"   14 1/2"

TRANSOM LAYOUT

3·2·2

1·7·1   1·7·1

1·1·4   1·1·4

G   F

2·6·2

STA. 3

C   D   B   A

2·2·5   2·2·5

4·5·2

JIG STATION MOLDS
SEE JIG PLAN ON SHEET 2

CLAMP
FRAME
7" at MID & STERN
7 3/4" at BOW
1/4" PLY SEAT
SCREWS INTO
FRAMES & RISERS
3/4" x 1 1/2" SEAT
FRAME
RISER

DETAIL of PLYWOOD SEAT N.T.S.

12 in   6   0   1   2   3 ft.
9   3

Sheet 2-4
Enlarge 257 percent for full-size plans.

The Scale Rule

Conversion Table

Boat	Model
1/8″	1/64″
1/4″	1/32″
1/2″	1/16″
3/4″	3/32″
7/8″	7/64″
1″	1/8″
1 1/4″	5/32″
1 1/2″	3/16″
1 3/4″	7/32″
1 7/8″	15/64″
2″	1/4″

The model is at a scale of 1 1/2 inches equals 1 foot.
Since 1 1/2 inches divides into 12 inches eight times (12 ÷ 1 1/2 = 8), the model is one-eighth the size of the boat.
Where the full sizes are given, divide by 8 to get the corresponding size for the model.

Because most of the boats in this book are built from full-size boat plans, the dimensions are given first for the full-size boat. In the text, I give that same dimension then (in parenthesis) the dimension for a 1 1/2 inches-to-the-foot model. Because many of these are such improbably accurate dimensions as 17/64, you'll probably find it easier to use an architect's scale rule.

For instance, I mentioned using a 1/4- by 1/4-inch stick for this skiff's stem. We get this measurement from the plans, where the stem measures 1 3/4 inches by 1 7/8 inches on the full-size boat, by using an architect's scale rule on its 1 1/2 inches-equals-1-foot scale. Like a computer, the architect's rule automatically converts *real* inches to *scale* inches (as long as you remember to use the correct scale), with absolutely no mental gymnastics on your part. This makes it easy to build a model to any scale from any plans for which dimensions are given. Just roll the rule over to another scale, and build away. It's all really quite simple; just thinking about it will probably keep you from nodding off in your chair, and may even help ward off early senility.

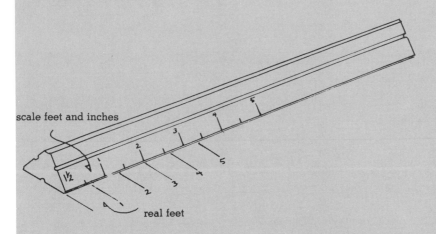

scale feet and inches

real feet

Let's Put Her Together

Glue the stem to one of the sides, leaving a quarter inch or so (a couple of inches in the full-size version, and $2 \div 8 = \frac{1}{4}$; see how easy it is?) hanging over both ends. Glue the transom frames to the transom, also letting them overhang both top and bottom. Place both sides upside down in the jig's thumb cleats, checking to see that the fore and aft position marks you made 2 feet $9\frac{3}{4}$ ($4\frac{7}{32}$) inches forward of the transom line up with the aft face of mold station 3. Stick pins through the sides to hold them there, or use micro clamps; glue the sides to the transom, and clamp or pin them in place.

Bring the sides in at the bow and glue them to the stem. If you find the thumb cleat slots on station 1 are so tight that they pinch the bend, relieve the slots, *not* the side of the mold. Make sure the sides come up slightly higher than the molds so they won't interfere with the bottom placement.

Sides and Chines

Clockwise from upper left: With the side panels located accurately on the jig, spread glue on the stem and clamp or pin the sides together....Notch the molds to receive the chines; trim the forward end of the chines to the stem's rake, and clamp them temporarily to the sides. Let them overhang the transom for now....Trim the chines to length with a razor saw held parallel to the transom framing. Now glue the chines in place....Saw the transom framing flush with the sides.

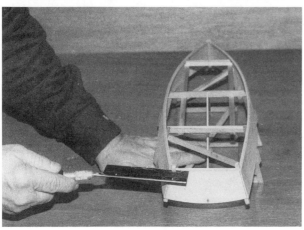

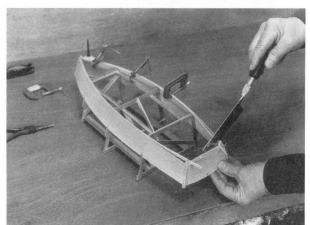

The chines go in next. Notch the molds in the way of the chines, but leave these cuts a little sloppy: you'll need to take the chine in and out several times during the fitting process. Starting at the bow, butt one chine against the stem end, pushing it down into the mold slots as you work toward the stern. Hook the aft end of the chine over the top of the overhanging transom frame and let the chine spring back against it.

Transfer the rake of the stem to the end of the chine, scribing with dividers or a pencil or scratch awl held on a block of wood—whatever works for you. Do the same thing to get the angle between the end of the chine and the side panel; make the end cut, and shore the chine against the stem to see how you've done. If you missed it a bit, a swipe or two with sandpaper across the end of the chine will bring it to size. Clamp the chine along until you get to the vicinity of mold 3.

We are now faced with fitting a tight joint against the transom framing, which is easier than you think. There are several ways to approach this; the easiest is to let the chine run by the transom and hook it against the transom frame. Hold your razor saw blade parallel to the rake of the transom and cut the end of the chine for a near-perfect fit, needing only a touch of sandpaper.

If you're interested in building the skiff full size and want to make your initial mistakes more affordable, or if you just like to do things in small scale the same way a boatbuilder works at full size, pick a straight-grained, knot-free stick about 3 or 4 feet long, lay it on top of the model's chine, and let one edge of it follow the inside edge of the side panel, right where the chine will lay. Butt the end of the stick against the transom framing right at the corner where the framing and side meet.

Without moving it either forward or aft, swing the stick onto the chine and mark this length. Since you now have the length of the chine right to the corner, for a tight fit you need only find the angle at its end. A bevel gauge will do it. Place it along the chine edge of the side and against the transom framing to get the rake cut, then against the framing for the transverse cut.

Make your cut longer and let the chine spring in. If the end of the chine cut is too tight, stick a wedge between the side panel and the chine to force the end of the chine just far enough from the frame so it won't bind when you saw it again. Do it this way and you've made a joint so tight that a razor blade couldn't enter. Whichever method you use, dry-fit the chines, then glue and clamp them in place—no fastenings needed.

Saw the bottom end of the stem and transom framing flush with the sides. With a miniature hand plane, take the outer edges of the chines down flush with the sides. Place a straight-edge across the chines to check their accuracy. They should be flat across to receive the bottom planks. Glue the stem cap on, leaving it long. The stem cap is made from square-edge stock and will be faired to the sides later.

Bottom Planking

Start planking at the bow, bringing the prebeveled edge of the first plank flush to the aft face of the stem cap. Mark the plank's shape and length of cut along the sides from below. With a razor saw, saw the planks to length at the same angle as the flare of the sides, leaving the marked line.

Make a sanding block from wood about ¾ inch by 2 by 5 inches. Cut a piece of wet-or-dry 220-grit sandpaper long enough to bring the paper over the ends, tacking it in place along the top so that the ends of the block are usable. Although we won't actually do any caulking, a cross-planked model looks peculiar without caulking seams. To create this effect, sand a slight bevel on one edge of each plank. Why not use a plane for this? Because a plane has a tendency to make seams too wide, too deep, and too irregularly shaped, not to mention

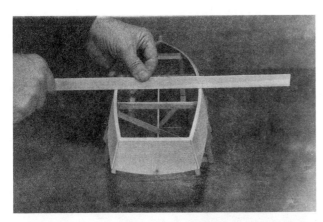

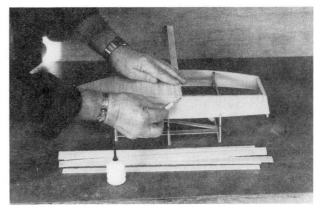

Clockwise from upper left: Trim the sides and chines flat across; check with a straightedge....Mark each plank and trim it to length as you go. Sand a caulking seam on one side of each plank. Glue only the *ends* of the planks to the chines and sides....Trim the drag strips with a razor saw held parallel to the sides.

that they can tear the grain, which often ruins the plank. Glue only the ends of the planks to the chines and the sides, even though some of their edges amidships might be above or below one another. They will even out later when we put the drag strips on, so not to worry. Turn the model over and, using a small, sharp chisel or the point of a knife, remove the excess glue at once. If you leave it, the glue will stain the wood and be difficult to remove later.

As you near the transom with your planking, lay out the last four or five planks in advance to see how they are going to finish out. You may need to take a little off the width of each plank to avoid having a peculiar-looking 1-inch wide plank to finish. It will happen every time if you trust to luck; Murphy's Law is ever watchful. Of course that's what makes boatbuilding interesting—model or full size. Completed boats are nice, but the challenge of building them is the exciting part. Sometimes Murphy wins, sometimes you win. You know you are making real progress when you win more often than you lose.

After she's planked, smooth up the plank ends with 60- or 80-grit sandpaper. Be careful about it; this coarse grit removes wood fast. Hold the sanding block at an angle so you won't leave scratches in the sides. Finish sanding with 220 grit and you will see all the beautiful endgrain patterns come to life. That's another reason I mix the different grain textures and colors. When varnished, the effect has real appeal, and it's so easy to do.

Drag Strips

The sectional view on Sheet 2-1—right under the skiff's profile —shows the three drag strips, which protect the boat's bottom. The center strip goes on first. Draw a centerline on the bottom from stem to transom, then measure the width of the drag strip and draw a parallel line to represent its outside edge; use this as a guide to keep the dragstrip running straight. Glue and pin it in place bow and stern. Now you can put a spot of glue under the dragstrip and push each plank against it to even their edges; this is why we didn't glue the plank edges during the planking process. The other two drag strips are 9 scale inches out from the center strip, so cut a 1¹⁄₈-inch long stick and use it as a gauge to mark a line exactly that distance from and parallel to the center strip. Put these on the same way as the center strip, checking their accuracy as you go with the stick you cut as a spacer. Trim the bow ends off the last two dragstrips with your saw held to the same flare and curve as the sides. Trim their aft ends flush with the transom and round them over with sandpaper (careful you don't scratch the transom). Since we aren't actually going to caulk the seams (we just put them in for authenticity's sake), we are done with the bottom. Now we can turn her right side up and finish her.

The four gunwales are 1¼ by ½ inches (⁵⁄₃₂ x ¹⁄₁₆) in the full-size version. The inside gunwales, or clamps, go on first and are fitted exactly the same way and in the same order as the chines. You will need only one micro clamp at the bow to hold an end in place; the fast-setting glue does the rest. Glue the outside gunwales in place, pinning their ends and, if necessary, using a few micro clamps in between. Trim flush the ends of the gunwales, stem, and transom framing.

The seat frames are next. These are 1¼ by ¾ inches (⁵⁄₃₂ x ³⁄₃₂), and have their tops tapered to ½ inch (¹⁄₁₆) so that they will fit flush under the clamps (inside gunwales). Start their taper (use sandpaper mounted on a block of wood) from the top of the seats. Cut them longer than needed, all at one crack, then fit them one by one on the sides where you previously marked their locations. Seat risers go in now, then the seats. Cut the seats a little longer and fit them by sanding their ends

Finishing Her Up

Left to right: Trim the seats to length and bevel their ends by rubbing them on a sanding block....Thinning varnish is the secret to a good varnishing job.

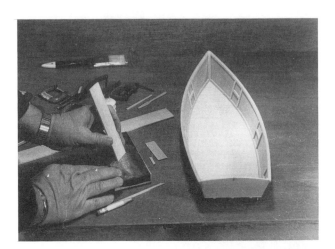

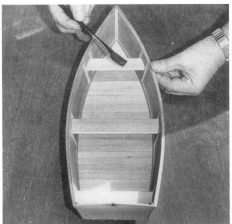

"Like a painted ship upon a painted...Toyota?"

and trying until they fit right. Glue the seats in, and look the model over for any uglies that need filling. Pinholes can sometimes be closed, or at least made smaller, by wetting a toothpick and pushing the grain sideways from opposite directions. This will raise the grain some but it sands off easily.

Fine-grained fillers and stains of about any color are readily available, but I chose to finish my model with varnish. I like seeing the wood's grain, it's the easiest to apply, and I can "doctor" it myself to my own specs. In this case, I thinned the varnish 20 or 25 percent with turpentine, and added a dollop of Japan dryer to speed drying.

Oars and oarlocks? Perhaps later, if skill and patience allow. Oars would be no problem, but oars and oarlocks sort of go together, so I don't want to make one without the other. To make a set of brass oar locks to scale might be a bit much now, but if you can't live without them, turn ahead to the Peapod Chapter, and go to it.

3

The Gloucester Light Dory

Dories may come and dories may go, but this one goes on forever. A classic . . . Prettiest two sheets of plywood I've ever seen." Praise for this little dory comes from everywhere. And well it should.

Besides its great looks, here is a boat that is sensibly constructed. Like the Gronros skiff, the Gloucester Light Dory is built upside down on its own jig, and the builder can put these beautiful dories together day after day without wearing out. With its light weight and clean-as-a-hound's-tooth interior, it's no wonder the plans sold for this boat have papered the world over. There's even a Russian version.

I'll show you how to build four different versions of this dory in small scale: a solid, "full" model; a fiberglass model; a half model for the wall; and a planked model, built just the same as the original. We'll start with the solid, full model; it's the easiest, and when you're done admiring it, it becomes a plug from which to clone a fleet of fiberglass dories for the mudpuddle set.

Materials Needed:

- a couple of 2-foot lengths of 4 x 4, or four pieces of dressed 2 x 4
- Weldwood Glue
- wood filler

Tools Needed:

- table saw
- bandsaw with a 1/2-inch tempered, skip-tooth blade, or hand crosscut saw
- drawknife, or an electric hand plane, small disc grinder, or jack plane
- spokeshave
- rasp (I like a farrier's rasp)
- scraper, such as a pane of glass
- roller to spread glue
- bevel gauge

The Solid Model

A visitor to my shop once asked Dave Dillion: "Dave, how do you tell people a simple way to take lines off a boat?" This is one of Dave's specialties, and he shot right back, eyes a-gleaming, "put it in a box, put it in a box."

A Plug in a Box

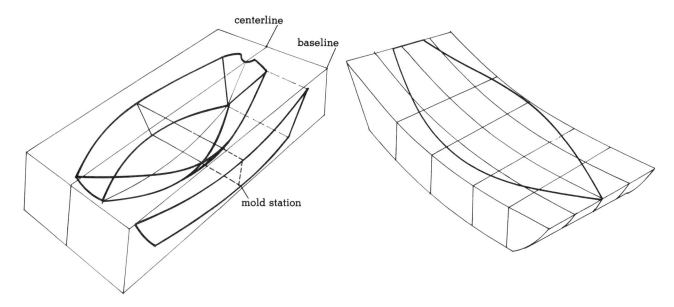

An imaginary box placed around an object has points of reference all around: top, bottom, sides, and ends. Using the walls of the box as reference planes, if you run enough slices through this object in the box you can copy almost anything as accurately as you want. Think of the box as three-dimensional graph paper and you've got it.

I won't give you a cram course in designing or lofting (if you want one, see Appendix A), but to build this plug you'll need to know that the starting point is the *baseline* (Sheet 3-1)—a simple straight line from which the designer determines the heights of different sections of his boat. Look down the center of your boat, and this same line becomes the *centerline,* from which the boat's widths are measured. Measuring down from the baseline and to each side of the centerline allows you to accurately position your boat inside the box—the rectangular chunk of wood that will become the plug.

The plug's *mold stations*—athwartships slices taken through the boat at measured intervals—are plumb and square to the centerline. On the plans (Sheet 3-2), the mold

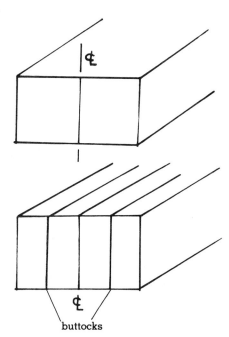

station heights (profile heights) are measured from the baseline, which runs along the boat's top. I used the top of the plug for the baseline and measured all the profile heights from it. Since I made my plug from four pieces of wood glued together, I used the center glue joint as the plug's centerline, and squared all the mold stations from it. Although new boatbuilders will want to get on to the curves, think plumb and square and a straight line first. Just as in housebuilding, these are the foundation of accuracy.

Getting Started

Looking at full scale (1½ inches equals 1 foot) plans, at station 4 the distance from the baseline to the bottom of the dory measures 3¼ inches. This is the minimum depth of wood needed to cut out the profile shape. You can make the plug by gluing together a couple of 2-foot lengths of 4 x 4; lacking that, use four pieces of dressed 2 x 4—as knot-free as you can find (regular, store-bought 2 x 4s, which actually measure only 1½ x 3½ inches). Either gives you a ¼-inch margin to spare.

Avoid knots like the plague. Consider building the model from almost anything to avoid them. I had some native cedar 4 x 4s on hand, scrounged from a local woodworking shop, but after eyeballing the sprinkling of knots with which they came equipped, I settled for gluing together four clearer pieces of dressed 2 x 4. For a plug, I'm not particularly interested in looks, but I am interested in accuracy achieved the easiest way. This means no knots to hinder progress.

Once you've found suitable wood, mix some Weldwood Glue (epoxy or other waterproof glues may be used as well), stirring it to the consistency of heavy cream. With 8 running feet of 3½-inch-wide 2 x 4 to coat, I used a roller to spread the glue; it puts on a fast and even coat. I did the gluing job on top of a piece of waxed paper placed on my table saw, since it is the only spot in my shop I know to be true and level. Why so fussy? If these pieces aren't lined up absolutely plumb and square at this stage, you'll never be able to build an accurate model later.

Roughing Out the Hull

By now I hope I've convinced you that the easiest way to build a model is with full-size templates—whether they're cut or traced from purchased plans, copies of plans, or plans you've drawn full size following the procedures in Appendix A.

With these plans in hand (and a pair of scissors in the other), cut out the profile view of the dory, right along the baseline. Go around the stem, along the bottom, around the transom, and back to the baseline. Lay the template on the side of your glued-up pieces with the baseline flush with the top of your wood, stick it down with masking tape, and trace around it. Take it off and repeat the process for the other side.

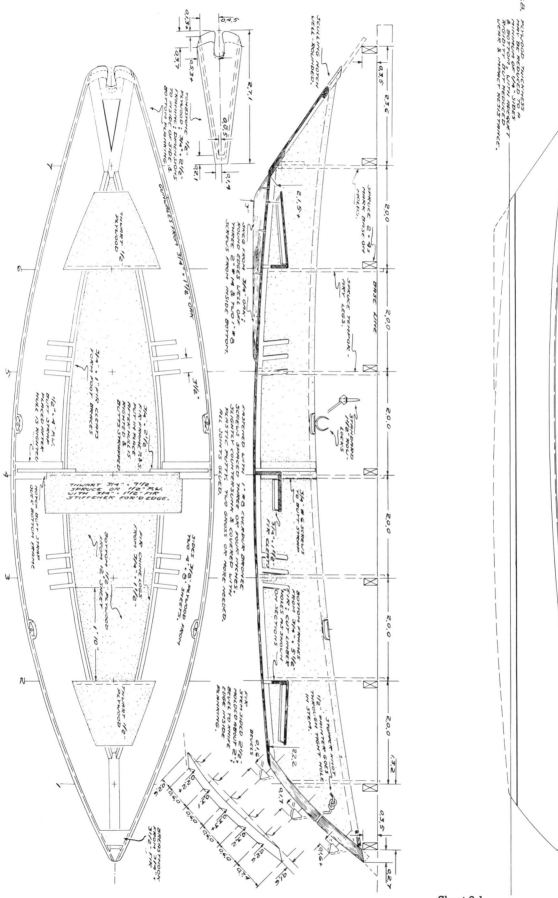

Sheet 3-1
Enlarge 281 percent for full-size plans.

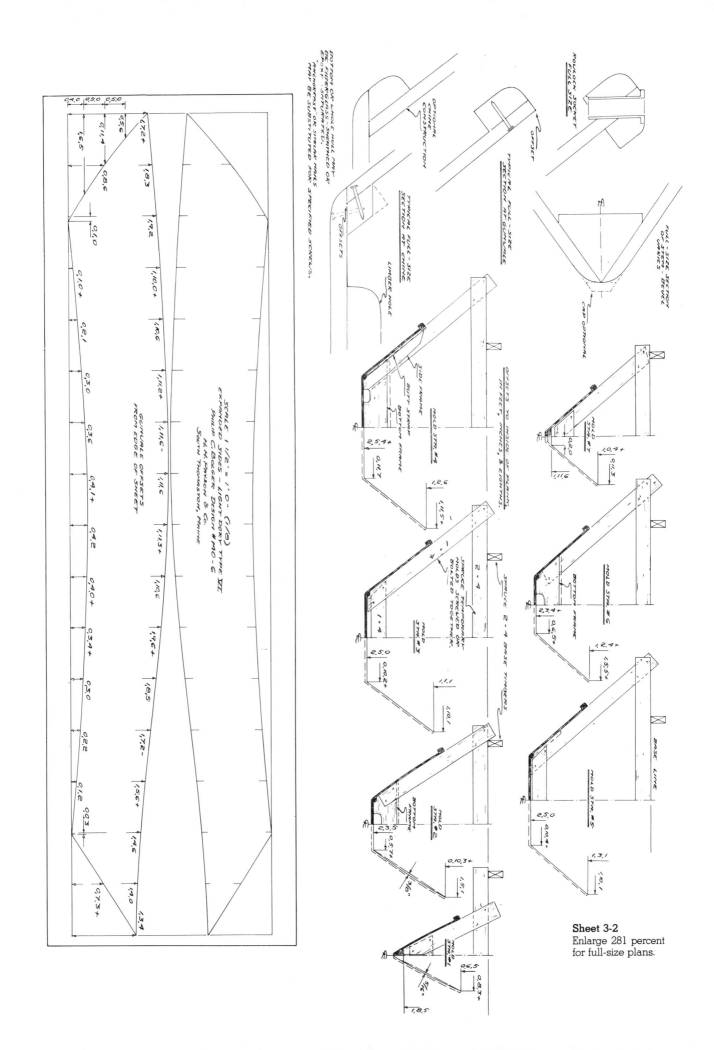

SCALE 1 1/2" = 1'0" (1/8)
EXPANDED SIDES - LIGHT DORY TYPE VI
PHILIP C. BOLGER DESIGN #140-6
H.H. PAYSON & CO.
SOUTH THOMASTON, MAINE

GUNWALE OFFSETS
FROM EDGE OF SHEET

POLLOCK SOCKET
FULL SIZE

FULL-SIZE SECTION
OF SIDES - BEVEL

TYPICAL FULL-SIZE
SECTION AT GUNWALE

TYPICAL FULL-SIZE
SECTION AT CHINE

OPTIONAL
CHINE
CONSTRUCTION

OFFSETS

LIMBER HOLE

CAP OPTIONAL

BOTTOM OR WHOLE HULL MAY
BE FIBERGLASS-SHEATHED OR
EPOXY-FIBERGLASS FILL.

"ANCHORFAST" OR SIMILAR NAILS
MAY BE SUBSTITUTED FOR SPECIFIED SCREWS.

OFFSETS TO INSIDE OF PLANK,
IN FEET, INCHES, & EIGHTHS

SPRUCE TEMPORARY
MOLDS SCREWED OR
BOLTED TOGETHER

SPRUCE 2-4 BASE TIMBERS

SIDE FRAME
BUTT STRAP
BOTTOM FRAME

BOTTOM
FRAME

BOTTOM
FRAME

MOLD STA. #4

MOLD STA. #7

MOLD
STA. #3

MOLD
STA. #2

MOLD
STA. #1

MOLD STA. #6

MOLD STA. #5

BASE LINE

Sheet 3-2
Enlarge 281 percent
for full-size plans.

Now *carefully draw all the mold stations completely around the box.* Cut out the sheer line from the template, being sure to leave on the tombstone's (transom) crown, place the profile template back on the wood, and finish marking the dory's top shape along the sheer on each side.

Take it to your bandsaw (if you don't have one, just keep reading) and cut the sheer profile shape first. Set your bandsaw's depth of cut to just over 6 inches. Don't use a 1/4-inch blade for this job; it'll cut a snake's path. The right blade for this job is a 1/2-inch tempered, skip-tooth blade.

Before you try to saw this stack of wood, think about it for a minute. Even if you walk hand in hand with God you're unlikely to hit the profile on the bottom, hidden side of the block exactly, so don't chance it. Instead, tilt your table so the blade will saw wide of the line underneath by at least 1/4 inch. This is easy enough to determine: line the blade up on the end of your box *before* you start cutting. Seeing *how* you're going to cut it *before* you cut it helps you avoid thinking one way and tipping the table the other.

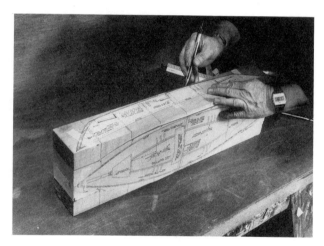

Left to right: Tape the paper templates to the block, trace around them, then draw the mold station lines completely around the box....Saw out the sheer profile.

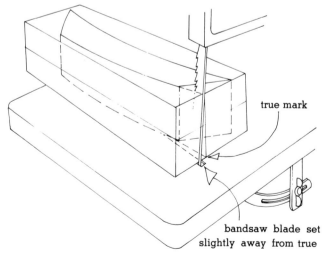

true mark

bandsaw blade set
slightly away from true

Be absolutely sure of this cut. You can lose the whole ballgame right here by trying to cut too close to an unseen line. It's far easier to take off the excess wood later by hand than try to put back what is no longer there. The same philosophy holds for cutting the bottom rocker, stem, and the stern profiles. Make sure the cuts toe out from the line—not in. These cuts should be done now, in exactly the same fashion as the sheer profile.

No bandsaw, you say? Just as we did with the little lobsterboat, substitute a hand crosscut saw. Make a series of cuts across the sheer line about ¾ inch apart, more and closer if you are ambitious (but be careful; don't make the cuts too deep). Chisel off the surplus wood between the saw kerfs with a spokeshave, block plane, and rasp (I like a farrier's rasp, more commonly seen filing horse's hooves), finishing flat across with a scraper, such as a pane of glass (wear gloves!).

Whether you've gotten this far with a handsaw or a bandsaw, a pane of glass does a good job of smoothing up all the saw marks, and can be cut wide enough to span the whole sheer. Be careful with sandpaper, though. You want nice crisp edges, so don't wallow your way carelessly across them.

Reestablishing the Lines

When you sawed out the sheer and bottom rocker you also sawed off the station lines, so you'll need to reestablish these on the plug, top and bottom. Pick up their location from the plans, draw them across and number them, then cut out a template of the plan view of the dory's top (plan view looking down, or a fish's view looking up—it's the same thing). Note that the station lines run outside the gunwales on the plans.

Lay the centerline of the plan view exactly on the wood's glued centerline. Surprise! The station lines don't match. Why? Because the plans were drawn on flat paper, but the sheer is now curved. No problem. Just place the template on station 1 and trace along it back to station 4; shift the template to station 7 and trace back again to station 4. She's the same length now and you only had to adjust the template about ¹⁄₁₆ inch each way amidships to do it—plenty close enough.

That's it for the top view. Now let's cut out the bottom template, following along the chine's inboard top edge. Look at the chines' projected ends on Sheet 3-1 and it instantly becomes clear which line you want. Use a ship's curve or a small batten to sweep in this curve on the template, where it is concealed by the seats. If you don't want to cut out the bottom template from the top-view template you just used, you can make a new tracing, or measure the bottom widths at each station and draw the shape on another piece of paper, using battens held in place with pins. Cut out this bottom template, lay it on your plug, and trace around it, keeping in mind that you will need to shift it fore and aft a fraction to allow for rocker,

Clockwise from upper left: After sawing out the sheer and bottom rocker, smooth them with a rasp and spokeshave.... Finish smoothing with a pane of glass....Reestablish the station lines on the plug; trace the top and bottom templates.

exactly the same as you did with the top template. You can cut out the tombstone transom if you want, but a couple of lines drawn from the chines to the top of the tombstone will work fine for now.

We've made it this far; let's not lose it now with an unthinking move. With the bottom's shape traced on the block, we are ready for the final cut. Since we are cutting from the top, the bottom line is hidden, so you must be sure the cut is well clear of the hidden line underneath. The procedure is exactly the same as when we cut out the sheer profile, with a wrinkle.

At first glance, it looks as if you can take the angle from number 3 mold, which has the greatest flare (39 degrees), and set your saw table's angle to, say, 32 degrees. This looks as if it should clear the bottom line at both that station and Station 7 (aft mold) by a safe margin.

But this pretty little dory has a surprise for the unwary: The sides have a 12-degree twist in their length. Number 1 mold flares 27 degrees; number 2 flares 34 degrees. If you set your saw to 32 degrees and make the cut you would wipe out the

The Final Cut

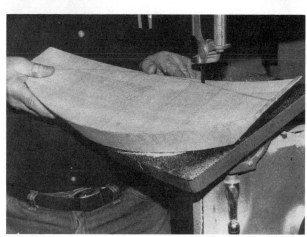

bottom at number 1 mold, and, if you're lucky, miss number 2 mold by 2 degrees. Instead, set your saw to 24 degrees and go to it; saw her full length, following the sheer line as close as you dare at that same setting. This leaves a safe margin all around.

The excess wood can be taken off quickly with a drawknife. If you haven't used one before, practice on scrap wood first. You need to pay close attention to the wood's grain, always being sure to cut down through the grain, rather than up against it. If you have no drawknife, you could use an electric hand plane, a small disc grinder, or a jack plane set coarse.

Clamp the plug in a vise, protecting it from the vise's jaws with sections of the scrap left over from cutting the sheer and bottom profile, and finish smoothing the plug with a block plane, spokeshave, and sandpaper. If you are real fussy—and why not be?—switch from 100-grit sandpaper to 220-grit mounted on a flat wood block. For the final touch, glue a 2 x 12-inch strip of 320-grit sandpaper to a flexible piece of wood and use it to

Clockwise from upper left: Taking angle from plans with a bevel gauge.... Checking angle on a bevel board—an easily made tool that belongs in the tool kit of everyone who builds boats—full size or models....Set your saw to 24 degrees and saw out both sides.... Remove excess wood with a drawknife. Practice on scrap wood first!

Finishing Up

take out the plug's slight humps and hollows. At the bow, note that stations 1 and 2 are slightly rounded between chine and sheer. This is a natural result of the rounded stem, so don't try to bring the sides dead flat here.

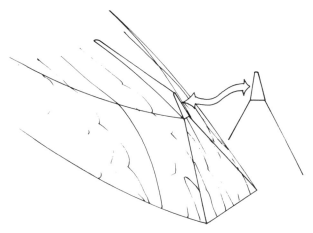

Left to right: Check the stem's profile with a template cut from scrap wood....Taper the skeg sharply.

To keep the outer face of the stem's profile accurate to a cat's whisker, trace its shape from the plans onto a piece of wood; cut away the stem, leaving its negative image cut into the piece of wood, and use it as a template. Look at the plan view and you will see that the end of the stem (stemhead) is about 1/8 inch across its face. Make the stem this width along its entire length, and keep the edges sharp for now. Before you can call the plug "done," you'll have to round off the stem and finish sanding it and the tombstone. A whack with a fingernail on a crisp corner can ruin the looks at this stage, so be careful about it. Cut out the skeg at least twice as wide as it shows on the plans, and taper it sharply to make the plug easier to remove from a fiberglass mold. I didn't taper mine enough and it got stuck the first time I used it. If you doubt your fiberglass-ing skills, don't put the skeg on at all. Without it, the dory's taper makes laying up a hull and pulling off a mold pretty simple.

Murphy Never Sleeps

I wouldn't want it any other way, but working with wood, especially cedar, has its surprises. So when I was sawing out my plug and a knot unburied itself nice and prominent right at the edge of the stem, I knew all was well. It looks like a hawse hole.

I can almost guarantee a hidden knot will surface right on the sheer line or on a sharp corner: wherever your eyes go first, whatever spoils a model's looks quickest. This happens so often you eventually become fatalistic about the whole thing and just keep going. After I pointed out a dragstrip gone askew on one of his plans, Phil Bolger replied, "If you don't make a mistake now and then, the gods are said to get angry."

At any rate, I filled the hawse hole with polyester resin mixed with microballoons I happened to have around. You can use Duratite wood dough, or polyester resin thickened with talc—almost anything fine grained and non–oil-based. Stick a piece of waxed paper over the hawse hole after you've filled it, and leave it there until the filler hardens. When you remove it, that former ugly will be as smooth as a pane of glass.

If you want, you can coat the finished plug with polyester resin (see below), wax it, and lay up a fiberglass dory right over it. The outside will be rough, but it's a quick way to clone one glass copy. But if you want to build a fleet, you've got to make a mold.

The Fiberglass Boat Business

We're not going to use a laboratory approach here; that's not my style. Besides, for a dory destined to be a flower pot, or dragged upside down through a mudpuddle by a kid, who cares?

Using Resin

Materials Needed:

• about 1 quart polyester fiberglass resin
• fiberglass hardener (MEK)
• acetone for cleaning tools (careful: this is nasty stuff)
• wax, automotive or the like
• about 2 yards 10-ounce (or 6-ounce) fiberglass cloth.
• colored fiberglass gelcoat (optional)

Tools Needed:

• cut-down milk cartons (for mixing resin)
• old paint brush
• scissors
• 3-inch roller
• knife
• rubber-faced hammer
• putty knife

Give your finished plug three coats of fiberglass resin. (You can pick this up at any marine store and most auto parts stores.) I like to use polyester resin: unlike epoxy, there's nothing fussy about it (including the price). My own recipe is a teaspoonful of hardener (MEK), or *catalyst*, to a pint of resin. About four tablespoons of resin will cover this plug, so I just guess at the amount of hardener—say 10 drops or so for this small batch. Sand lightly between coats, being sure to allow ample drying time. The first coat of resin will sink into the wood and, because it's a thin coat and thus prone to slow drying, it will probably stay tacky, especially if the temperature is below sixty degrees. If this happens, and you think it's never going to set up, or if you wonder whether you got enough hardener in it, don't worry. Give it another coat with a little additional hardener, keep the temperature warm, and it will set up fine.

After the resin hardens, wax the plug with four or five coats of wax, allowing it to harden up a bit between coats. You can use automobile wax for this, or you can use mold release wax if it's handy. I've tried two or three different kinds, from Butcher's to Rain Dance, and they all seem to work OK on a small job like this.

Pros do the mold layup with the plug upside down, and so will we. Because they plan to pull a good many boats from the mold during its life, the pros are pretty serious about their technique. Their molds are made with the plug's sheer laying on a flat surface. This produces a glass lip or flange that stiffens the mold and provides a reference for trimming the laid-up hull. That's fussier and more time-consuming than we need, so we will simply lay up the mold over the plug and trim the excess glass flush with the sheer *before it hardens.*

Laying Up the Mold

We can lay up both the mold and the hull using ordinary 10-ounce fiberglass cloth. This is the most commonly found weight, but if you have lighter cloth on hand—say 6-ounce—don't worry about it. Go ahead and use it; just use more of it. Five layers of 10-ounce cloth (or eight layers of 6-ounce) makes one tough mold.

Attach the plug upside down to a scrap board, using nails or screws driven through the board and into the plug, or double-faced tape. You want to be able to work freely around the plug. Lay a scrap piece of cloth over the plug, and with a dry paint brush, brush the cloth out in all directions. If the cloth has a selvage edge, cut it off to release the weave's directional restriction. Lay the cloth right over the skeg (if you ignored my warning and put one on) and keep brushing until the cloth fits around the hull like a glove.

When you're satisfied with the fit, cut around the hull's sheer with scissors, leaving about 1/2 inch of overhang every-

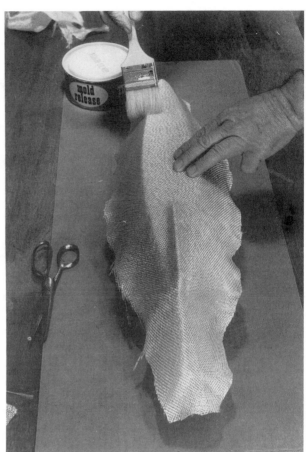

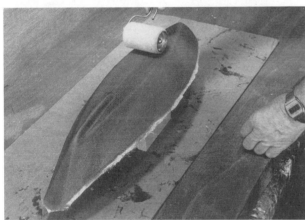

where. Take the cloth off the plug and, using it as a pattern, cut four more pieces for the mold and three for the hull layup. If you're planning to build a fleet, you may want to transfer the first piece of cloth's shape to a cardboard pattern.

Mix up about a quarter-pint of resin. Lay a piece of cloth on the hull and, starting with the bottom, brush on resin, working out from the middle in an ever-widening span. At first the cloth won't behave, wrinkling and refusing to mold around the stem, but keep at it, brushing the wrinkles from different directions. When you get the cloth completely saturated, it'll do what you want.

As I mentioned earlier, glassing over the skeg is the hard part; Murphy really shines here, so beware. You'll have to slit the cloth lengthwise along the top of the skeg to release entrapped air. Get rid of any interfering cloth and replace it with loose strands of fiberglass mat (mat consists of short, randomly-oriented strands). Build up this skeg area without wasting time, then lay on another layer of cloth right away, again paying particular attention to the skeg. After several layers are on, you can lay the rest of the cloth right over the skeg without

Clockwise from upper left: Coat the plug with resin....Sculpt the cloth to the plug with a dry brush....Wet out the cloth with resin; add succeeding layers without delay. Even out the resin with a roller after all the layers are in place.

Left to right: Trim the fiberglass flush with the plug before the 'glass hardens completely....Free the plug from the mold by alternating tapping and prying.

cutting it. When the last layer is in place, use a 3-inch roller to even out the resin in the cloth for a good-looking job.

Let the laminate set up for an hour or two, checking the curing process periodically. Before it becomes rock hard, take a knife and trim the cloth flush at the sheer all around the hull. Too late, you say, it's hard as a rock? Take it to your bandsaw (or use a sabersaw), trim it as close as you dare, and sand it flush with the plug.

Now for the fun part: getting it out. Will the plug come clear of the mold, or is it stuck forever? Tap around the hull with a rubber hammer, then, anywhere along the sheer, insert a putty knife between the mold and the plug. Work it along, and you will see the color of the mold change. This is air entering between the glass and the plug, indicating separation. Slip the putty knife around both sides, whack along the bottom with your rubber hammer, and the mold should come free. If it doesn't, something is stuck.

Mine stuck along the skeg (Murphy!), but with a screw eye in the plug for leverage and with my wife holding the mold, we managed to break the two free—unfortunately destroying the skeg in the process. I had to dig it out and reshape the skeg cavity some before I could lay up the hull. Lesson learned: Next time, make the skeg much wider, and sharply "veed." As I said earlier, I could have just left the skeg off and spared myself the anxiety, but I found it somehow more satisfying to mold the boat and skeg together at once.

Wax the inside of the mold three or four times, waiting between coats to let it harden up a bit, then give the mold a couple of coats of gelcoat, the color of your choice. (I like Coast Guard Orange—also known as International Orange. You can see it for miles, which is why fish draggers usually painted their dories with it.) Let the gelcoat harden up just a little shy of rock hard before you start the layup. (Colored gelcoat sets up slower than clear resin so I add a little more hardener to the mix.) Commercial fiberglassers apply gelcoat with a sprayer, which produces a nice even coat, but gelcoat is really hard on the type of small sprayers average modelers have around their shop, so a brush will have to do.

If you've kept the skeg as part of the mold, you can expect that the cloth won't go down into the skeg cavity any easier than it would go over it, so dump some resin in it and stuff in some strands of matting or roving to strengthen it. Then lay the three layers of cloth right over it, this time without cutting it anywhere.

Laying Up the Hull

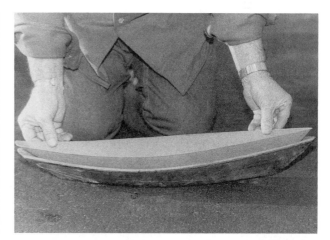

Clockwise from upper left: Lay up the hull in the mold over the almost-hard gelcoat....Remove the cured hull from the mold the same way you removed the mold from the plug....Bear-boat chartering in South Thomaston, Maine.

To recap, lay up the hull with three layers of cloth, starting with a brushed-on coat of gelcoat against the waxed mold, filling the skeg cavity, then laying the cloth against the gel-coated surface. (You can skip the gelcoat if you want, but it makes for a nice finish.)

The procedure for extracting the finished hull from the mold is the same as that for freeing the mold from the plug. If you want to fancy up the hull a bit, add a gunwale, and maybe seats if you want (see "Finishing Up" the planked model, later in this chapter). Add a string to tow her with, and look around for a kid and a puddle.

Building a Half Model

Building the wooden plug for the glass model was fun, but building a half model is just as much fun and half the work. They make elegant wall decorations, especially if mounted on a piece of varnished mahogany or other contrasting wood. If you understood how to make the wooden plug, then making the half model will need little explanation. You use the same cut-up plans, photocopies, or tracings for templates, but cut them in half lengthwise along the centerline, between the sculling notch and the stem.

You can vary the hull construction to suit your own taste and available materials. You could use lumberyard 2 x 4s and paint (don't forget to paint the waterline, it adds a lot). Or you can get fancy and build the hull from the waterline up with some pretty wood; make the part of the hull below the water-line from a contrasting wood; then sandwich a strip of mahogany veneer between the top and bottom halves. Var-nish it up and you've made yourself one pretty model. This little dory is one of the few boats that looks good from any angle. If you come close at all to capturing her looks you've got a winner.

Left to right: The half model is just that: the plug split down the centerline. Make the bottom and waterline from contrasting slices of wood....Mount your completed half model on an attractive board and hang her up.

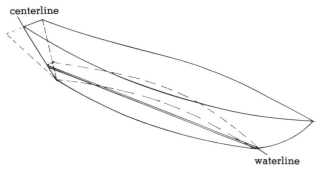

centerline

waterline

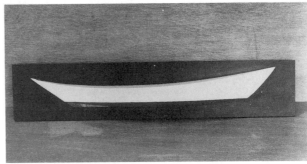

Building the Planked Model

Another, and perhaps the most rewarding way to build this dory, is to make a planked version of it. We'll build this model much as we would the full-size version, but with some variations to make the job easier.

Back in their heyday, fishing on the Grand Banks in the late 19th century, dories were built right side up, starting with the bottom—a hard way to go I'd think. No chines were used, and their lapstraked sides (like clapboards on a house) were edge-nailed into the bottom and to the closely spaced frames. One of those constantly leaking old Banks dories was my first real boat. I got it secondhand when I was a kid for all of $5, which I had earned picking blueberries.

This dory is 100 percent different from the old-timers. It's built upside down on a jig; it has only one frame (amidships); the sides are one piece, as is the bottom; and both sides are fastened to chines. That's a considerable improvement over the ever-leaking, split-out edges of the old dories' garboard planks. You can elect to build this model with or without chines, so the procedure varies slightly with the method you choose. When I first built a bunch of these models way back when, I went the no-chines route, because the flare of the sides and the rake of the stem and transom make the chines inaccessible for fitting or wiping up spilled glue. If you want chines in your model (maybe you're planning to build a full-size dory and want to make your mistakes small scale), bevel them top and bottom 38 degrees; clamp them in place; flatten them across, then put the bottom on. But I suggest you first try building this model without chines.

In a nutshell, here's the basic, no-chines procedure we'll follow for transforming flat, cut-out pieces into a completed

Materials Needed:

- 1/2" (or so) plywood - 6" x 26" (or so)
- 1/4- or 3/8-inch plywood scraps
- 1/8" x 6" x 26" plank stock—plywood, cedar, spruce, whatever
- a few strips of contrasting hardwood, about 26" long
- varnish
- turpentine
- Japan dryer

Tools Needed:

- table saw
- razor saw
- hammer
- bevel gauge
- scale rule
- block plane
- dividers
- small, round file
- 80-, 220-, and 320-grit sandpaper
- 5/8" brush

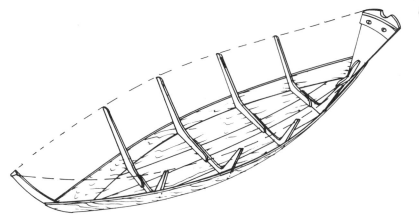

Old-time dory construction.

hull: Build a jig; place the stem and transom on it; glue the bottom to the stem and transom; bend the prediagrammed, precut sides (see Sheet 3-2) around the jig; and glue them to the stem, the transom, and the edges of the bottom panel.

Now to get this dory a-building we need to set up a jig to hold the seven mold stations. It's much easier and quicker to make the base and the mold stations from solid wood, rather than using the (scale) 1 x 4 and 2 x 4 construction shown on the plans. Why? Because solid pieces don't go out of shape as a bunch of sticks are wont to do. Granted, there is a loss of artistic beauty, but so what; it's just a building form. As usual, I went the easiest route, and used a piece of 1/2-inch plywood 6 by 26 inches for my base. You can make it thinner or thicker—whatever you have on hand.

Draw a centerline on your base; mark off the mold stations right square across, just as you did when you made the plug. Cut out templates for each mold station from the plans (be sure to cut *inside* the plank line), cutting along the *outside* edge of the temporary molds, then along the *bottom* of the cross brace to the centerline. You'll end up with a half section. Lay this pattern on a piece of 1/4- or 3/8-inch plywood, trace around it, then flip it over and draw the other half of the mold.

Carefully cut out the molds, and glue and nail them in place right along the base's centerline, making sure that molds 4, 5, 6, and 7 are forward of their station marks and molds 1, 2, and 3 are aft of theirs. By locating the molds this way you can saw them out square-edge, no bevel. Because only their faces sit on the station marks, they occupy no more room than the drawn line. If you paid no heed to which side of the mark you put them, they would stick out like a sore toe, keeping the planks from bending around the jig in a graceful curve. You knew that? Well good! Beginning boatbuilders are often told to do this, but seldom told why.

Now we need to make a support for the stem and tombstone. Cut out a template from the triangular section of the plan defined by the baseline, number 1 mold, and the aft face of the stem. Trace it onto a piece of wood no thicker than the stem (1/8 inch), and stick it in place right on the centerline of the jig. Repeat the process for the tombstone's support block, cutting out the triangular section of the plans defined by the baseline, the forward face of the tombstone, and the aft face of station 7.

Cut a notch in the stem support, down next to the baseline, to receive the clamp that will hold the side panel in place while the glue sets. The aft tombstone support needs a scab of wood pinned temporarily to its sides for your clamps to grip while they hold the tombstone in place. What size clamps you use

Building the Jig

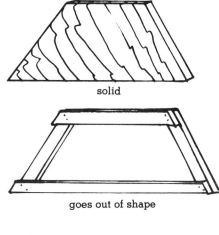

solid

goes out of shape

half mold

Stem and Tombstone

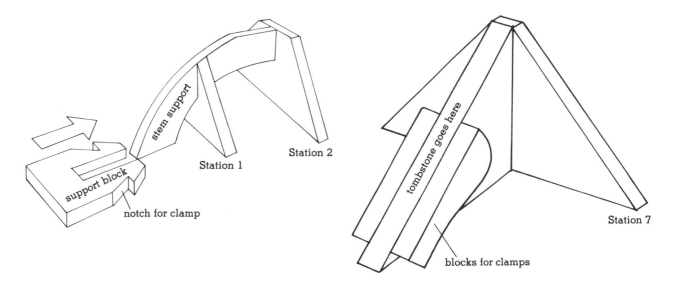

Left to right: Stem support....Tombstone support.

directly affects how you'll make these clamp supports, so you're pretty much on your own here.

You can make the tombstone without framing if you wish, but I think framing looks sharp, so I used it. Cut out the tombstone pattern (note that the *outside* line on the plans is the *inner* face of the framing), extending the lines well past the top, so that the tombstone ends up being an inch longer than shown in the plans.

Why? The shape of the sides when they're bent around the jig determines the accuracy of the whole show; they must follow a fair curve. You can slide the stem and tombstone up or down a little to accommodate the lay of the sides, and you won't hurt the accuracy one iota; try it the other way and it will drive you nuts. Those big, long sides lie where they want, so do yourself a favor by making the transom and stem longer than shown on the plans. With this model, as with all boatbuilding: "If it's there you can always cut it off; if it ain't, you're in trouble."

Bevel the tombstone and its framing 42½ degrees and put it in place; add the piece of wood for the sculling notch later when you cut that lovely crown into the tombstone's top.

Lay the stem profile pattern on a piece of wood (watch the grain) a strong (scale) 5/16 inch by 4 or 5 inches wide by 5 feet long (3/64 x 1/2 or 3/8 inch x 7½ inches), and cut out the *face* of the stem. Strike a centerline on it, roughly bevel the stem about 30 degrees for starters, then cut it clear from the block. Place the stem on the jig and check the stem's bevel with a batten sprung around the jig's molds 1, 2, and 3. This shows you exactly how much more needs to come off the stem to permit the side panels to flow around the jig and land on the stem in a fair curve. A small, notched block of wood will hold the stem

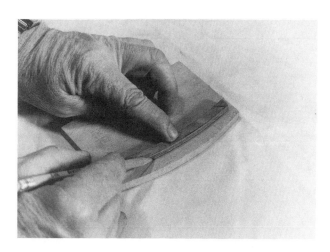

Left to right: Tracing the stem. I'm using a plywood pattern here; you'll probably use one made of paper....Cut the stem's heel flush with the stem support.

in against the jig, but don't glue it down: you'll need to slide it away from the stem when your dory comes off the jig.

Fasten a small, square batten (a *sheer batten*) below the sheer marks on both sides of the jig to guide the sides and hold them in place while you fasten them to the stem and tombstone. A couple of thumb cleats on molds 3 and 5 that you can drop the sides down into will work just about as well.

The Sides: Easy or Educational

The sides go on next, but first we have to determine their shape. You can use the pattern I've provided (Sheet 3-2); just add ¼ inch to the bottom edge so that it will cover the bottom planking and give us some leeway for fitting. That's the quickest and easiest way to plank the sides, but you won't learn much by it. If you feel up to a challenge, you can do it the same way as many professional boatbuilders—one of the easiest and most accurate methods of *spiling* I know. Learn it and you can drink with the masters. (If you're not ready for spiling, and just want to get on with the model, skip this section for now. But plan on coming back; spiling's a skill worth knowing.)

The Art of Spiling

Cut a piece of scrap wood a scale 1½ inches by ¾ inch (3/17 x 3/32), long enough to run the length of the jig and a little beyond. Spring it around the molds below the sheer batten, making sure it lies flat to the molds *with no edge set.* Let the ends of this plank touch the ends of the sheer batten, then mark the ends of the plank by eye or with dividers. To ease the spiling job, we want to cut off some excess wood here to enable us to move the plank a little closer to the sheer batten.

Now set your dividers to the greatest space between the edge of the plank and the sheer batten. With the leg of the dividers resting on the sheer batten and the pencil resting on

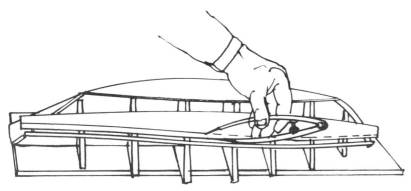

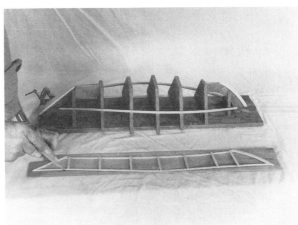

Transferring the shape of the sheer batten to the spiling plank with dividers.

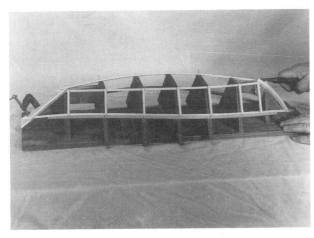

the plank, trace along the entire length of the sheer, thus transferring the sheer line to the plank. That's what you call spiling.

The chine edge is spiled pretty much the same way, except there's no batten to spile to. Instead, use tick marks at each mold, made on the reverse side of the chine batten. Connect the dots with another batten, cut it out, and there's your chine. Lock the spiled sheer and chine together with cross ties at each mold, and you have your template. Add about 1/4 inch to the bottom edge as mentioned earlier, and you're ready to cut out the plank.

Left to right: Connect the sheer strip and the chine strip with cross pieces....Trace the side pattern's shape on the plank stock.

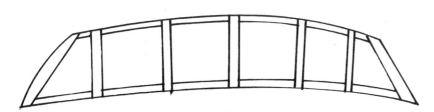

But why do it this way, you ask? Why not just spring a batten along the sheer and chine marks, wrap the plank stock around them, and mark their shape directly from the battens? Well, it *can* be done that way, but there's no room for your fingers to work a pencil behind the molds on this model. Besides, learning several different ways to do one job is good for your gray cells.

Now suppose you decide to spring the chine and sheer battens around the molds, lock them together into a template, and lug the template to a sheet of plywood for marking. You transfer the template's shape to the plywood, cut it out, and it doesn't fit within a row of beans. What happened? The template sprung out of shape the second you took it off the jig. Why? Because the battens released the spring you put in them when you forced them around the molds; that's why you keep hearing "don't edge set the batten" if you are going to use it for spiling.

The safe way to make a template that has to be moved is to make a spile fit to both edges and lock the two together. Then you can move it around all you want. To boil it all down: Be sure your template flows naturally along the shape you want to take off—twist and all—but allow *absolutely no edge set.*

Here's still another, even easier method. Suppose you have whittled out a model of a 12-foot, flat-bottom rowing skiff. It has straight sides, perhaps with a little flare and a bit of twist, and you want to find out quickly what the shape of the sides will be so you know how wide a plank you'll have to buy.

Wrap a piece of light cardboard or stiff paper around the side of the skiff and trace the side onto it. Take another piece of cardboard or stiff paper with two straight edges and two square ends, and mark it off at spaced intervals, using whatever scale suits. Plop the side template on it, trace around it, measure in along each of the intervals, and read off the measurements for making the plank's shape.

To find the width of plank stock needed, draw two parallel lines snug to the top and bottom edges of the side template. Measure across and there's the width of stock you need to get out your plank. Transfer the template measurements to your plank stock and there you have it.

Planking the Bottom and Sides

As I mentioned before, we are building this model a little differently from the full-size boat: The bottom goes on before the sides. You can use the bottom cut from the plan as a template, or you can spring a couple of battens around the chine marks on the molds and mark the bottom planking directly from them. Either way, cut it a little wider than needed, trim off the edges of the stem and transom, and glue on the bottom.

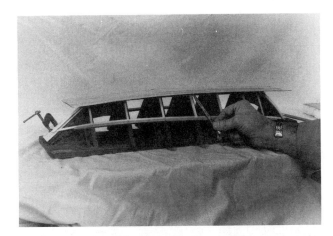

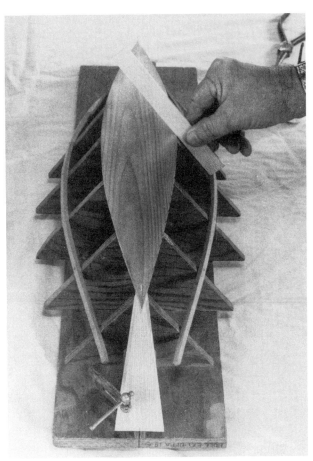

Trim the bottom to size and bevel its edges to match the flare of the molds.

The sides and bottom can each be made from a single slice of wood (1/8-inch thick; use a sharp planer blade in your table saw), or from two pieces edge-glued together. This is the way I did it; I wanted to try my hand at mixing and matching grain, adapting what I had lying around to the job at hand.

Try your side template against the jig to see that it has enough depth to cover the edge of the bottom panel (it's a good idea to leave the aft ends of the sides a bit long, too). Cut out the sides and try them for fit, being sure to allow overhang everywhere. When you're satisfied, draw a relocating mark bisecting the side and bottom so you won't have to guess where the side goes when you are ready to put it back on for good.

This is a good time to mark the location of the seat risers on the side panels if you haven't done it already. Note that on the plan view (Sheet 3-1) the forward face of the stern thwart risers lands on the aft face of mold station 6; the aft edge of the amidships seat risers lands on the forward face of mold station 4; and the forward thwart's after face lands on the forward face of mold station 2.

Clockwise from upper left: Trace the bottom's shape on the planking....Check the bottom's bevel with a straight edge against each mold....Trace the bottom's shape on the side planking; cut it oversize and trim after installation.

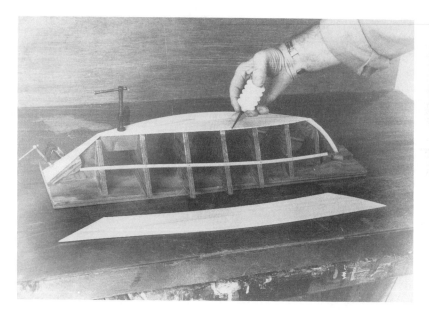 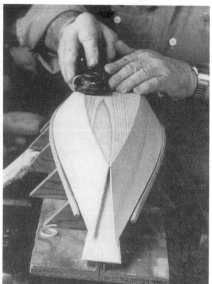

With your side panels all marked and trimmed to shape, spread some glue on one side of the stem, the edge of the bottom panel, and the edge of the tombstone, and put the first side on for good. A clamp or a pin at the bow near the top of the stem, and a clamp or two at the transom, are all you need to hold the side in place until the glue grabs; finger pressure is enough to hold it against the edge of the bottom panel. Wait half an hour or so before taking off the bow clamp, then put on the other side. Trim the excess wood from the bottom along the transom and stem, but don't round any edges; leave them sharp for now.

When you remove the dory from the jig, the sides will want to pull together slightly. So before removing it, mark the locations of mold stations 2, 4, and 6 lightly on the outside of the hull, right up next to the sheer. Cut spreaders equal in length to the width of these molds at the sheer, and hold them in place with a pin stuck through the hull, just below the path of the gunwale. Keep the spreaders in the hull until after the thwarts and gunwales are in place.

You can either round off the stem, sanding it smooth, or cap it with a *false stem*. I made both the stem cap and the gunwales from mahogany. The contrast between the varnished cedar hull and mahogany stem and gunwales is quite striking.

To cap the stem, finish the face of the planking at the stem flat across, then cut out a square-edge stick wide enough to

Left to right: After fitting the side, spread glue on the stem, tombstone, and the bottom's edge, and put on the side for good. Don't get any glue on the jig, or your dory will be on the jig for good....Trim the sides flush with the bottom using a small block plane.

Finishing Up

easily overlap the edges of the planking. To help it bend, wet the stem cap's outside face with your tongue, then glue and pin it in place. After the glue dries, fair it to the sides. This is the safest way to do this job. You're spared the agony of finding out, after the glue is dry, that your carefully prefitted stem went a little askew and doesn't quite cover the edge of the planking.

After the stem cap is faired, put the gunwales on. Although their finished dimension is 3/4 by 1 1/2 inches (3/32 x 3/16), they go on easiest if they're cut from wider stock to follow the top shape of the side panel pattern, laid flat. This uses more lumber and looks strange, but take my word for it, it's true. Boatbuilding is full of optical illusions like this, but hang with it and you will learn them as you go; it's part of the fun. The gunwales should have their undersides beveled 30 degrees—easy to do on the table saw—and have their ends trimmed flush with the tombstone and stem.

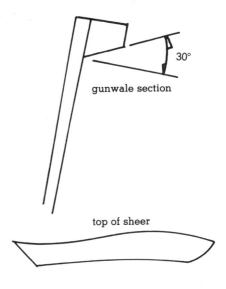

gunwale section

top of sheer

Cut out the skeg and, for a good fit, place a piece of sandpaper on the bottom panel where the skeg goes. Rub the skeg back and forth, fore and aft, until it hunkers right down "humming tight."

Insert the wedge of wood that supports the scull notch, and mark the tombstone's crown on both its faces. Cut off the tombstone's excess wood with a razor saw, making the cut from the aft face (the safe way to do it), then file the scull notch to suit with a small, round file.

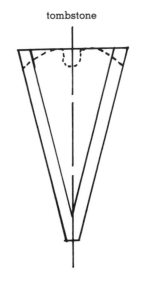

tombstone

Put in the seat risers and seat tops and she needs only the foot stretchers to complete the job. These are the little upright cleats on the sides—six aft and six forward; 1 by 3/4 by 8 or 10 inches (1/8 x 3/32 x 1 or 1 1/4)—that you brace your feet against for hard pulling. If making 12 of these little toothpicks individually seems like too much trouble, you're right. Make the job easier by sawing out the whole batch at once. Cut a couple of sticks long enough to make them all, with some to spare. If you figure on coming out just right, chances are that the last one will have a flaw in it, which you will not spot, of course, until you throw out your jig and set up your saw for some other job. Place half a dozen of these cleats side by side and round their ends together. Cut their bottoms at 40 degrees with the razor saw—just guess at it—and hit them with sandpaper if the angle isn't just right. A simple jig works wonders for spacing them symmetrically in the hull—much faster than trying to align each one to a pencil mark by hand.

Do the final sanding of your model with 320-grit sandpaper; get the dust off, give her four or five coats of thinned varnish, and you're done, although you may want to make a simple cradle to display her properly.

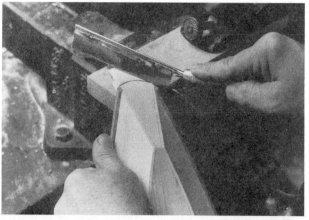

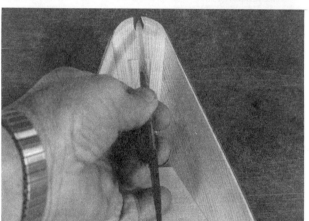

If you liked the model, and you take a notion you want to build this dory full size, you might consider buying *A Classic in Plywood: How to Build the Gloucester Light Dory* (Wooden-Boat Publications, 1982).

Back in 1964, Phil Bolger said "causing rowboats to be built is a godly and pious act to be duly rewarded in the hereafter." If this holds true, his "pet," the Gloucester Light Dory, ought to ensure his reward. When he gets to the Pearly Gates and St. Peter asks, "What's your excuse?" Phil will say, "I designed the Light Dory." St. Peter will have to let him in.

Clockwise from upper left: Glue and clamp the fitted gunwales in place....Cut the arc in the tombstone's top....File the sculling notch to shape.

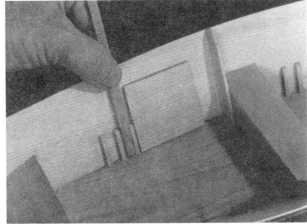

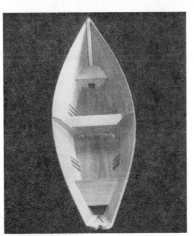

Clockwise from upper left: Round the tops of the foot stretchers with a sanding block, all at one crack....Space the foot stretchers with a jig; don't rely on your eye or bother with measurements.... The finished product....Make a cradle to display her properly.

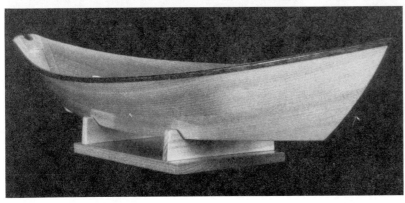

Phil Bolger's key to the Pearly Gates.

Sea Hawk, an outboard-powered semi-dory, is built about the same way as the Gloucester Light Dory. But when it came time for me to build a construction model of her, the material I chose was something else again: Formica. I remember being desperate for something to build the model from, but there was no hobby shop in town where I could buy thin plywood. Then some scraps of Formica I had lying around the shop caught my eye.

At the time I was working winters after lobstering was over, putting in kitchens to make a buck, and I noticed how easy it was to bend the Formica I'd been using for countertops—no humps and bumps. But a Formica boat? Why not? It bends around in one big, beautiful, fair curve; contact cement sticks it together (exactly) where you put it, so you don't have to worry about sliding joints; a table saw, Skilsaw, bandsaw, or even a scratch awl, all cut it with ease; edges can be easily planed, filed, and sanded. You can buy odd shapes and sizes dirt cheap at hardware stores and lumberyards. Not bad, when you stop to think about it.

If you're short on materials for any of these boats, or if you've just had a kitchen installed and can't bear to throw out all those forest green Formica scraps, consider using it to plank a model. It's not the most pleasant material I've ever worked with, but I've seen worse. And the price is right.

A Formica Boat?

The marbleized Formica dory.

4

Bobcat—An Instant Catboat

I first met up with this little gem while thumbing through a copy of *Small Boat Journal*. She was in Phil Bolger's cartoon section, a part of the magazine devoted to producers and dreamers alike. With her cocky sheer and boottop waterline, this salty looking, gaff-rigged craft caught my eye, and I had to have it.

When the plans arrived, my eyes went right to that full bow. Could I really twist the bilge panel enough to land it where the plans showed? What shape would it finally take? How much plywood would I need to lay out two of them?

What better way to answer all these questions than by making a model? A model of the easiest kind, using techniques I learned from an article by nautical architect Weston Farmer, way back in the early days of *National Fisherman* (later reprinted in *From My Old Boatshop*, IMP, 1979). I wanted a model of *Bobcat* that showed her lines—never mind the interior; a model I could pick up and eyeball all over; one on which I could work out in small scale and at small cost what could otherwise be very expensive, both in time and money, if done full size.

We'll build *Bobcat* this same, simple way, in the same 1 1/2-inches-to-the-foot scale we've been using right along; and we will use the same building technique: full-size templates.

Materials Needed:

- 1/16" x 12" x 4' plank stock
- 7/16" dowel
- wood glue
- masking tape
- pins
- thin strips of contrasting wood
- scraps of copper flashing

Tools Needed:

- bandsaw, jigsaw, or sabersaw with a fine-toothed cutting blade
- small block plane
- razor saw
- table saw
- accordion-style glue applicator
- bevel gauge
- drill bit the same size as your pins
- ignition point gauge or extra-small bevel gauge
- needle-nose pliers

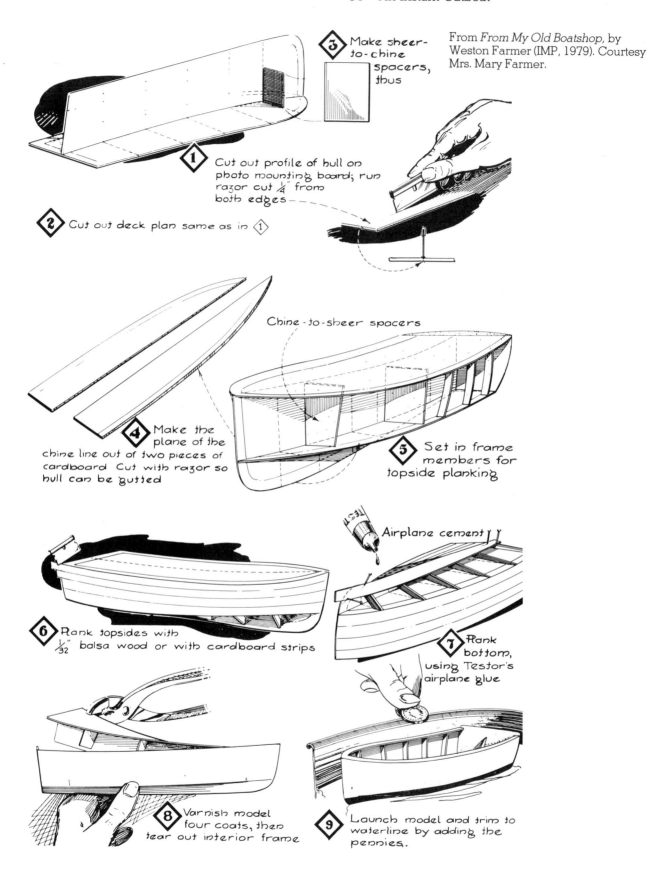

From *From My Old Boatshop,* by
Weston Farmer (IMP, 1979). Courtesy
Mrs. Mary Farmer.

3 Make sheer-to-chine spacers, thus

1 Cut out profile of hull on photo mounting board; run razor cut ¼" from both edges

2 Cut out deck plan same as in ①

Chine-to-sheer spacers

4 Make the plane of the chine line out of two pieces of cardboard. Cut with razor so hull can be gutted

5 Set in frame members for topside planking

Airplane cement

6 Plank topsides with 1/32" balsa wood or with cardboard strips

7 Plank bottom, using Testor's airplane glue

8 Varnish model four coats, then tear out interior frame

9 Launch model and trim to waterline by adding the pennies.

If I seem to harp on using templates, it's for a good reason: It is so easy to mismeasure. Architects do it, engineers do it, we all do it. A phone call I got while writing this chapter takes the cake, however. The bewildered builder said: "I'm building *Nymph,* and the frame tops don't come within three inches of meeting the sheer."

Now *Nymph* is a tack-and-tape boat, just like *Bobcat,* and Bolger's plans make laying out these Instant Boats as easy as can be. Everything is laid out on 4 x 8 sheets of plywood. Because plywood comes with reliably square ends, you don't even need to use a framing square. The edge of the plywood serves as the baseline, and all measurements are made from it in an orderly fashion.

"Frames measure OK in height?" I asked.

"Yep."

"Sure?"

"Yep."

"What about the sides, how did you measure them?"

"I measured from the edge of the plywood to the sheer, then from the sheer to the bottom of the side panel."

"OK, I see what happened. The plans give you both measurements, but you aren't supposed to move your rule once you've hooked it over the edge of the plywood." He measured from the edge of the plywood *to* the sheer, then measured again *from* the sheer, making one pregnant-looking panel. It's no wonder the frames didn't come to the top.

"So what am I going to do with these sides? I've got them both cut out," he said.

"If you've got the top right, do the bottom again. If nothing's right, you'll have to start over from scratch."

I never heard from him again. I can only assume everything came out all right. Or he gave up in disgust.

On With The Model

What materials should we use to build this little catboat? Just about anything. If you want a bright-finished hull you can saw your own stock to size, using whatever you have on hand or the wood you like best: spruce, pine, cedar, basswood—just be sure it's straight grained and knot-free. The plans call for 1/4-inch thick planking for the full-size boat. At this scale, however, that means 1/32-inch planking—tricky to rip, and the

Material Options

model would be too fragile. Instead, shoot for a scale 1/2-inch thick (1/16 inch) planking for the sides, bottom, and bilge panels.

If you want a painted hull, store-bought model-aircraft plywood is a time saver. You can saw all the parts for the hull from a 1/16-inch thick, 1 x 4-foot sheet—$8 at this writing. If that's too rich for your blood, you can even use cardboard.

Weston Farmer used cardboard for the model I saw in *National Fisherman,* and for a couple of the models in his book. He wasn't specific about what *kind* of cardboard, though, so I grabbed the first stuff that looked as if it would do the trick— cheap stuff you find in new shirts—and my first model didn't look like much.

Recently a reader called saying he had photocopied the plans for a tack-and-tape dinghy from one of my books, cut out templates from the photocopy with a razor blade, and stuck them onto cardboard with glue stick. He used "file" cardboard for the sides, bottom, and bilge panel, and thicker, photo-mounting board for the frames and transom. After cutting out and assembling the pieces, he was pleased enough with the results to call and tell me about it. This is one of the things I enjoy most about this book-writing business: It's a two-way street. My readers learn from me and I learn from my readers. If you're short of wood or just curious, you can use the same materials and techniques for *Bobcat.* Painted, it won't look half bad. You may be hard-pressed to tell the difference.

Templates First

As always, we begin by cutting out paper templates of all the boat's parts. This simple building method begins with a longitudinal member that doesn't exist in the full-size boat: a profile of the entire hull, traced or otherwise reproduced from the construction view (Sheet 4-3), including stem, transom, bottom profile, mast location, and sheer. This is the *strongback,* or spine of your model.

Cut out your paper template for the strongback along the outside of the stem, following along the bottom *inside* the planking, (the heavy line along the bottom in Sheet 4-3). Cut off the skeg. Cut *outside* the transom, then back along the sheer *under* the deck (dashed line abaft the centerboard, heavy line forward) to the stem. Next cut out frames A, B, C, D, and E (Sheet 4-1) *inside* the planking, leaving them solid to the top of the sheer. Cut out the transom (Sheet 4-1), then the bottom and side panels. To avoid edge set, cut out the side panel along the baseline, then cut around the ends and bottom.

You can decide here whether you want to go the easiest route possible: glue the paper templates directly to the wood, cut out around them, and leave the templates in the boat. If you

Using a scale rule to measure plans....Cut out paper templates for all *Bobcat's* parts....Be sure to leave the line intact when cutting out templates.

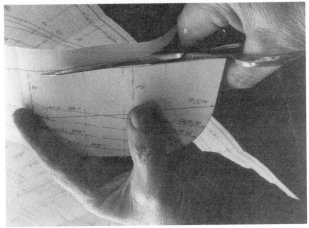

wish to reuse the templates, trace around them onto the wood with a *sharp* pencil. A dull pencil mark equals about 1/8 inch at this scale. Trace around a few templates with a dull pencil and the accuracy of your model will be irreparably harmed.

Getting Out the Parts

Start with the pattern for the side panel. Small, narrow pieces like to edge-set out of shape, so cut the template bigger to start with. The trick is to mark one edge then cut the other; put it back on the wood and finish tracing. I use this method every time for long, narrow pieces, and it works. Lay the template on your wood, smooth it fore and aft with your hands to get out any wrinkles, and lay a weight on it to hold it still while you're marking around it. Trace around the bottom and around the ends, then cut off the excess paper along the sheer. Lay the template back on the wood and trace along the top.

Be sure to mark the locations of the station frames on the side panel; we must know where these go so we can build an

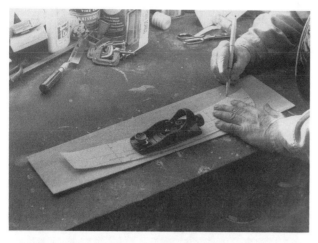

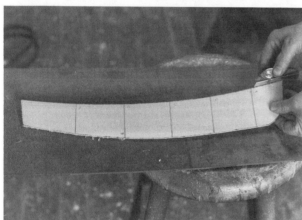

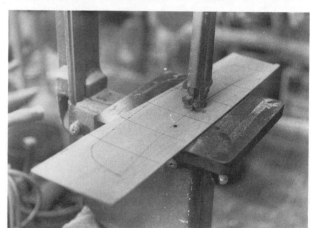

accurate model. Do the bottom panel exactly the same way (again, be sure to get the station locations marked correctly). The bilge panels need no station locations; they just fill space between two fixed points. Cut the bilge panels well clear (1/16 inch) all around their marks to give yourself some leeway for fitting later.

Mark centerlines on both faces of the frame stations and transom if you haven't done it already. Ignore the limber holes; you want these corners left on to help align the panels.

Cut out all the boat's hull parts using a fine-toothed cutting blade in your bandsaw, jigsaw, or sabersaw. If you're unsure of your sawing ability, give yourself a break and trim to the line with a small block plane. Notch the backbone to receive the frames later, cutting down from the top of the sheer just past the center. Notch all the frame stations the same way, but from the bottom up. These notch cuts should be slightly ·loose to allow the model to self-adjust.

Glue two small sticks to the backbone on each side of the mast's profile to guide the slotted heel of the mast to the proper

Clockwise from upper left: Trace the template's shape onto wood; use a *sharp* pencil....Mark the locations of the station frames....Cut out the parts with a fine-toothed saw; leave the line intact.... Trim to the line with a small plane.

Bevel the transom by rubbing it across sandpaper held flat. Note the markings for the centerline and tiller cutout.

rake (take the angle of the rake directly from the plans). Cut a 1/2-inch deep slot for the mast down from the top edge of the backbone. Add a couple of beveled cheek pieces (you can take the bevel directly from the plans) to the backbone at the stem to give more bearing for the sides and bilge panels.

Clockwise from upper left: Take a slice off the backbone equal to the transom's thickness, then glue on the transom. Slot backbone and frames; make cuts a bit oversize....Add beveled cheek pieces to stem. Cut a slot for the mast; reinforce its sides with four small sticks.... Fasten the frames and backbone together temporarily with pins....Pin the first side panel temporarily in place.

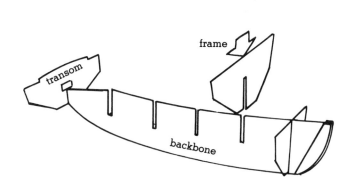

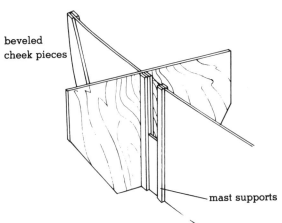

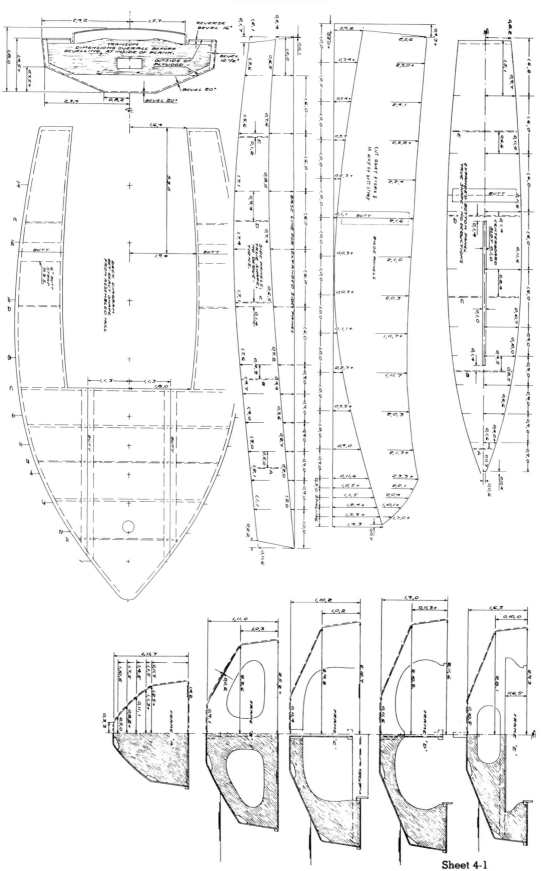

Sheet 4-1
Enlarge 367 percent for full-size plans.

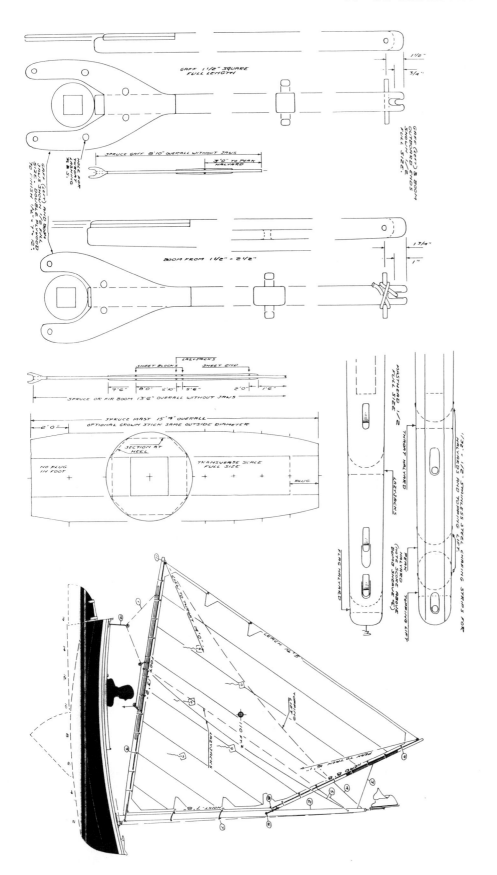

Sheet 4-2A
Not to scale.

Sheet 4-2B
Enlarge 736 percent for full-size plans.

Sheet 4-3
Enlarge 367 percent for full-size plans.

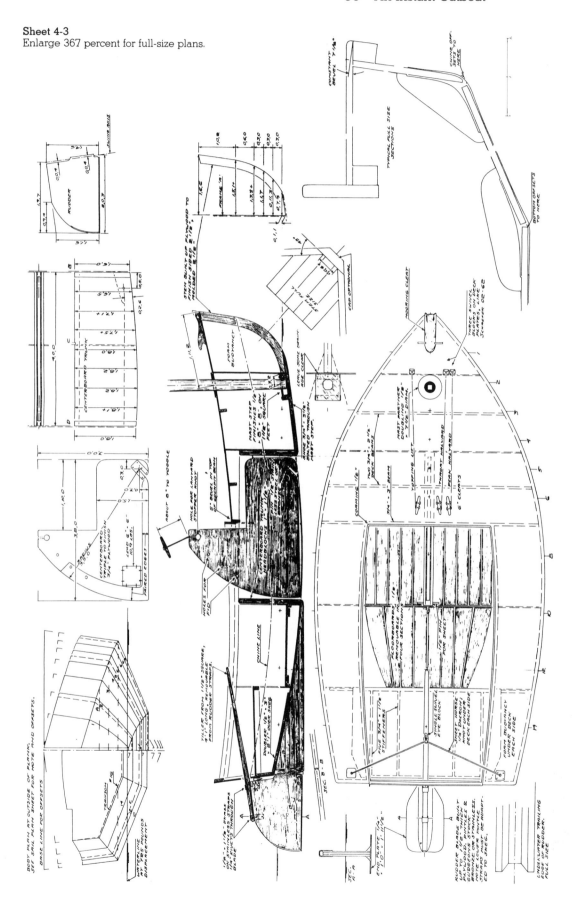

Bevel the transom as shown in the plans; cut out the tiller hole, but don't bother to frame it. Take a slice equal to the transom's thickness off the backbone's profile now, before assembling the model. This keeps the backbone the exact length needed for the sides and bottom panel to bend around, so don't forget it.

It's Time for Assembly

To stick her together, we want a needle-nose, accordion-type glue dispenser filled with either Franklin Titebond or Elmer's Carpenter's Wood Glue. The dispenser will help you get into tight places and lay a bead of glue right where you want.

Because the transom's centerline will be hidden when you glue it in place, draw a line parallel to it to represent one-half the thickness of the backbone. Be fussy here; you don't want your transom cocked off-center when someone admires your handiwork. Glue and pin the transom to the backbone, then place each frame station (no glue yet!) in its slot.

When your glued-on transom is set firmly, pin the two side panels to it and to each of the frames (no glue yet!). Make sure the tops of the frames are flush with the top edges of the sides along the sheer. Work the side panels along until they land on the beveled faces of the stem, making sure they are both the same height; if all is well, glue them in place. Now glue the sides to the transom, making sure that all the frames lie perpendicular to the backbone, then glue the sides to them.

Mark another line parallel to the centerline, just as you did with the transom. Spread glue across the bottom edge of the transom and along the backbone; then, with its centerline resting squarely on the backbone, apply the bottom panel. Adjust the frames to lie straight and square across the bottom panel, then glue them to both the bottom panel and along the backbone slots, so that everything locks together.

A Tricky Fit

Now that the side panels, the bottom panel, and the transom are all glued in place, all that remains is the pair of bilge panels—"whiskey planks," as the old boatbuilders used to call them, because the last planks to close her in often were celebrated with a tot of rum or whiskey. If you get it right, you may want to resurrect the custom.

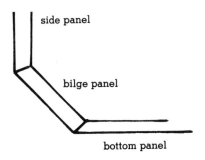

This is the tricky fit. Cut the panels a little wide (they're already laid out a little long in case you miss the end cuts), and think of an orange slice as you bevel these panels, carefully working your way along their edges, sanding a bit here and there as necessary to get a seam you're proud of. Draw a line across both panels at the seam to relocate the bilge panel in

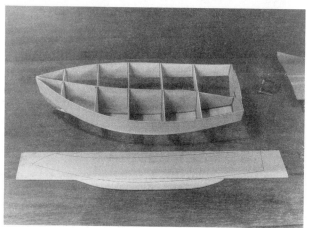

the exact same spot each time you remove it for trimming. Hold it in place with masking tape during the final sand-and-fit stages.

Apply glue to the edges of the frame panels, the transom, and the beveled stem faces, and fix the bilge panel in place with pins and masking tape until the glue dries. Repeat this on the other side; trim the ends of the bilge panel flush with the transom; glue on a stem cap (use cedar, pine, mahogany—whatever comes to mind and bends), and your catboat hull is completed. Chances are if you got this far with the model, you could build her full-size.

Clockwise from upper left: Adjust the side panels and frames until everything is fair. Glue the side panels in place.... Fit the bottom panel, fastening it temporarily with pins. When everything is adjusted, glue it in place....Bevel the edges of the bottom and side panels to mate with the bilge panels....Cut the bilge panels a little oversize; trim to fit with the panel in place.

relocating
line across panels

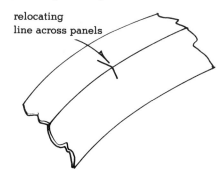

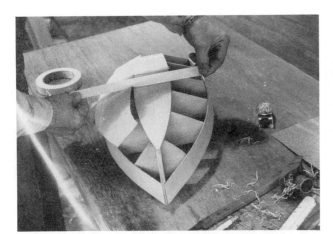

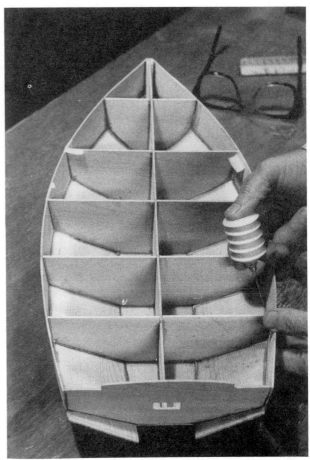

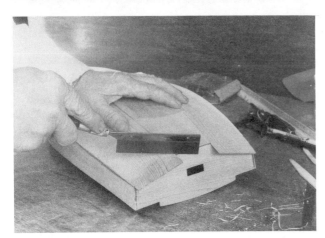

Clockwise from upper left: Tape bilge panel in place while fitting....When everything is shipshape, fasten the whole works together with fillets of glue applied to all mating surfaces....Trim the bilge panels to length; be careful not to scratch the transom with the razor saw's teeth.

For the Mantel

Building a model this way is a straightforward approach to get a look at the hull lines and understand a boat's construction. But add a deck, a coaming, a mast, and a skeg and rudder, and she really shapes up, elevating her to mantelpiece status.

Cut out a pattern for the skeg from Sheet 4-3 and lay it out on 1½-inch (3/16-inch) stock. Add the sternpost as shown, sand the skeg to fit (lay a piece of sandpaper on the hull where the skeg is to go, and rub the skeg across it from side to side for a quick-and-easy fit), and glue it in place. Make the rudder in the same way, and the same thickness as, the skeg, adding a plate made from as-thin-as-you-dare wood to its underside. The

plate gives the rudder bite when she is heeled hard over, a nice feature for tubby catboats, whose excessive beam makes them prone to lose steerage in sudden wind gusts. I made the rudder straps from ordinary copper flashing, scraps of which are available from any tinsmith's shop. (If you can't find one where you live, try a building supply store.) These were bored for and pinned to the rudder. Gudgeons and pintles were made from common pins; no attempt at fanciness here.

Trim the backbone to clear the tiller where it enters the slot in the transom. The tiller is tapered at its aft end so that it may be unshipped easily from the metal straps (copper flashing again) that hold it to the rudder. Taper the tiller first, then adjust the straps to fit and pin them in place.

Make a pair of gunwales from $^3/_4$ x 1 inch stock ($^3/_{32}$ x $^1/_8$), bevel their tops 7$^1/_2$ degrees to align with the deck, and glue them on. Sand the frame tops, the edges of the side panels, and the gunwale tops together so they are flat across and ready to receive the deck.

Cut out the deck pattern from the plans and lay it out on wood, leaving a safe margin all around for fitting and planing. If you are manufacturing your own wood you could use a few edge-glued strips for the deck. If you use cedar or another light wood for the rest of the deck, the *king plank* (the center plank in the deck through which the mast is stepped) would look nice if made from a darker shade of wood, say mahogany or cherry.

Think about things a bit before you cut the hole in the deck for the mast. The mast is raked aft—the sides of the hole are plumb, but the ends are raked—so you can't cut the hole square to the deck. Take the mast's angle from the plans with a small bevel gauge, such as an automotive ignition point gauge, then, using it as a guide for your drill, cut the hole through the deck.

The mast is round and tapered at both ends; the full-size

Left to right: Make a stem cap from a contrasting wood and glue it in place. Fair it to the sides later....Fit the skeg and rudderpost to the bottom by rubbing across sandpaper.

gudgeon and pintle

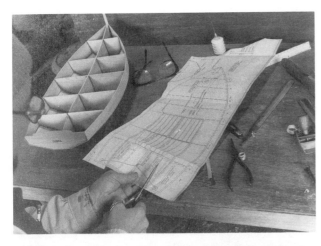

Clockwise from left: Cut out a deck pattern from the plans....Glue the deck in place. Make the king plank from a contrasting wood, or stain it a different color....Mark the mast's location (take the angle of rake directly from the plans).

Add all the goodies. Make the coamings and gunwales from thin, contrasting wood. File the Jonesport mooring cleat to shape with needle files. Make its cross bit from a brass pin cut to length. Make the rudder straps from scraps of copper flashing.

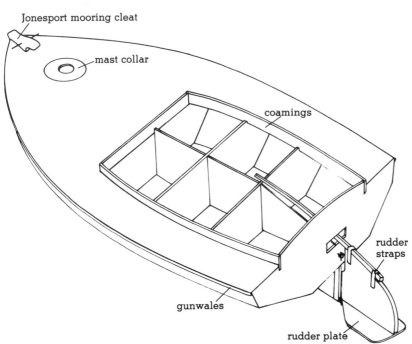

Jonesport mooring cleat

mast collar

coamings

rudder straps

gunwales

rudder plate

Add a smooth finish, paint her waterline (see Chapter 5), make a simple cradle, and *Bobcat's* ready for the mantel.

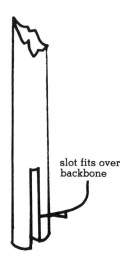

slot fits over backbone

edition is hollow. For the model, I passed up the hollow part in favor of a solid stick of no special heritage—it certainly wasn't Sitka spruce. Other than rounding it, putting in a little taper, and cutting a slot for it to slip down over the backbone, I paid it no special attention. I made no gaff or boom, nor did I bother with any rigging.

To keep the mast from warping, you might consider splitting it, rather than sawing it, from a two-foot piece of straight-grained pine. The mast should finish 15 feet 4 inches by 3½ inches at the partners (23 x $^{7}/_{16}$), tapered at the top as shown in the plans. Split the mast over-size (you may need to do several to get one good one), taper it, eight-side it (plane it to an evenly tapered stop sign along its length), then round it with sandpaper. If all that sounds like more trouble than it's worth, just pick up a $^{7}/_{16}$-inch dowel from the hardware store, taper its top with sandpaper, and call it good.

Finish off the deck with a mast collar, the Jonesport mooring cleat, and coamings made from thin scraps of wood—preferably a contrasting hardwood. Fair the edges of the deck flush to the gunwales, round them off, and the woodwork on this model is complete. To scribe her waterline, see how it's done in the next chapter.

Make her a cradle, give her four or five coats of varnish, and *Bobcat's* done. In the next chapter, we will build her petite sister, *Cartopper*, and fancy her up more. Instead of using a slotted backbone and sticking in solid frames to get her shape, we will cut all the pieces from the plans and make a miniature of the real thing—hardware and all. This means more work, and a bit more skill, but the reward is well worth it.

5

Cartopper

It's unlikely that designers will ever devise the perfect boat for every occasion and sea condition, but still they have fun trying—and the quest is likely to keep them busy forever. And all-purpose boats *are* popular, especially those suitable for shallow-water cruising. Here in rocky, tide-swept Maine we have deep water galore. But south of here it's all sand, sandbars, and shallow water, and that means kickup rudders and centerboards. With them, you can sail right up on the beach and step out dry-footed anywhere.

Looks, light weight, and all-around performance are built right into this newest Phil Bolger tack-and-tape design. Her sprit rig, centerboard, and kickup rudder allow you to enjoy effortless, shallow-water cruising; should the wind fail she'll take you home nicely under oars or a tiny outboard.

This isn't the first all-purpose boat Phil designed for me. The 15-foot *Gypsy* was another, and as her owner John Garber put it: "Her spare plywood frame has all the structural elegance of a bird bone, or the inside of a green pepper." But not, unfortunately, their light weight. When I watched John struggle *Gypsy*'s 150 pounds up on top of his van here in my yard (he wouldn't let me help), I thought a car-top version of her was long overdue. Phil agreed and *Cartopper* was born; so now let's build her small-scale.

Materials Needed:

- six or so slices (cut extra) of straight-grained wood, 1/16" x about 2½" x 19"
- 3/32" and 1/4" x 6" x 12" (or so) slices of wood
- wood glue
- scraps of sheet brass and lead flashing
- 1/4" dowels
- small machine screw and two nuts
- a teasponful of polyester or fiberglass resin
- scrap of 1/16" brazing rod
- brass pins
- thin twine, about 1/32" in diameter
- thinner twine, about 1/64" in diameter
- an old spark plug

Tools Needed:

- table saw
- bandsaw or scroll saw with a fine-toothed cutting blade
- small block plane
- small tap-and-die set (optional)
- jeweler's saw
- razor saw
- vise
- emery board
- small bevel gauge
- sandpaper
- small twist drills
- modeler's ball peen hammer
- set of small files
- small try square

Getting Started

We skipped building *Bobcat's* interior because our main interest was to see her lines in the flesh, so to speak. This time, however, we'll go whole hog and do it all: a kickup rudder, a weighted centerboard with an honest-to-God chunk of lead, a mast and sail—the works. It will take more skill and time, but the results will be worth it.

Cartopper's plans are drawn 1½ inches equals 1 foot. Sheet 5-1 shows the layout of her hull parts: the side panels, bottom

The Plans

panel, bilge panel, transom, rudder, rudder cheeks, center-board trunk, and foresheets. Sheet 5-2 shows in enlarged detail the construction of the centerboard, the stem, transom bevels, and a body plan looking fore and aft amidships. (You can ignore the table of offsets.) Sheet 5-3 shows hull construction in profile and plan view, her three frames, and her floor platform. Sheet 5-4 shows her spar dimensions and sail plan, with a choice of a 59-square-foot leg-o'-mutton rig, or a 61-square-foot sprit rig. To further simplify things, Sheet 5-5 is a full-size pattern for *Cartopper*'s three frames, which you can trace directly from this book.

As usual, we will start building *Cartopper* by making paper templates of all her parts and transferring their shapes to wood, beginning with the side panels (Sheet 5-1). To avoid edge set, cut out the side template along the straight line that runs right over the top edge of the uppermost panel on the plans, then cut along the panel's ends and bottom. Lay the template on your wood and mark around the bottom and ends, then finish cutting out the template along the sheer. Now put it back on the wood and finish marking its outline.

The Bilge Panels, Bottom, and Transom

Clockwise from upper left: Trace the side panel template's shape onto the wood....Mark the frame's locations.... Cut out the side panels....Cut out and frame the transom. Cut the bevels with sandpaper mounted on a block of wood.

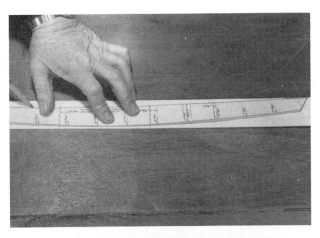

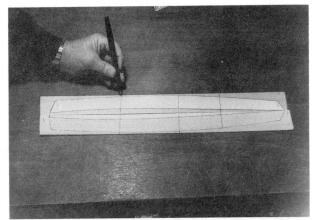

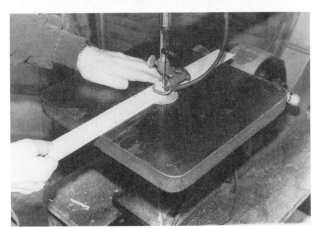

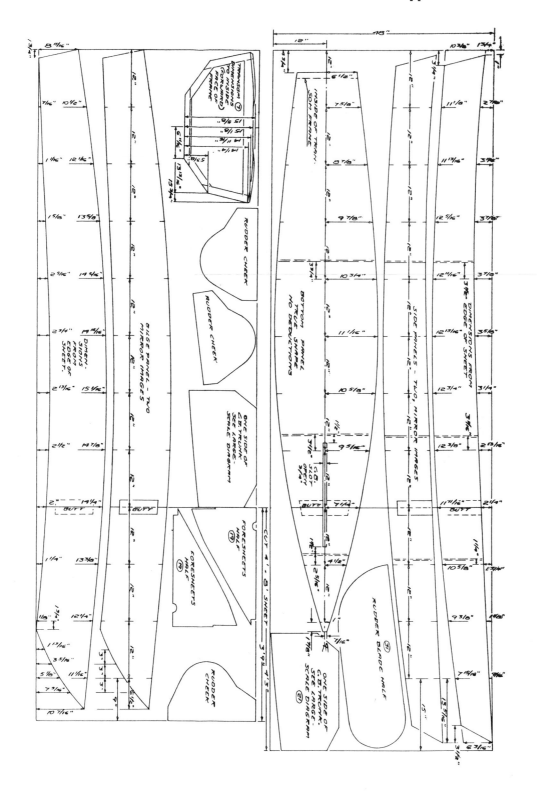

Sheet 5-1
Enlarge 250 percent for full-size plans.

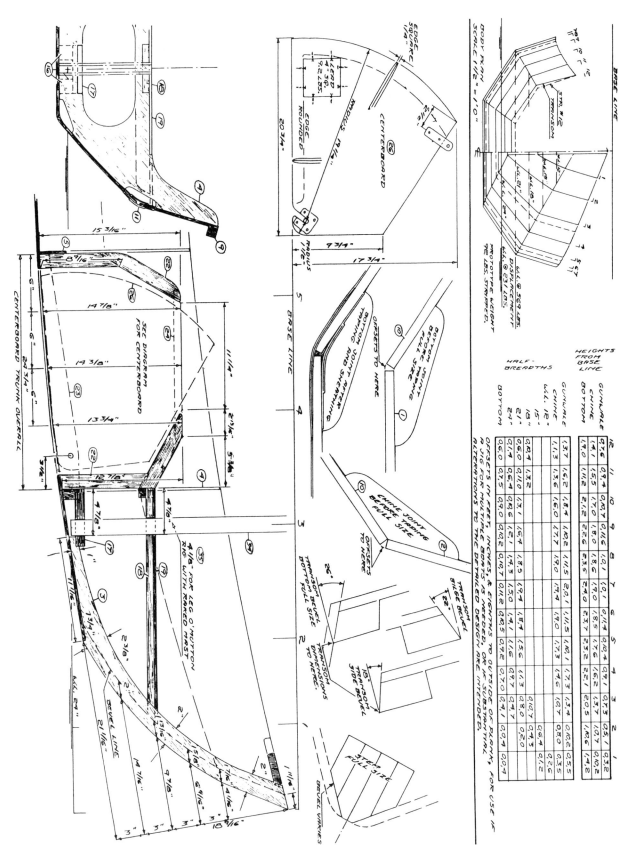

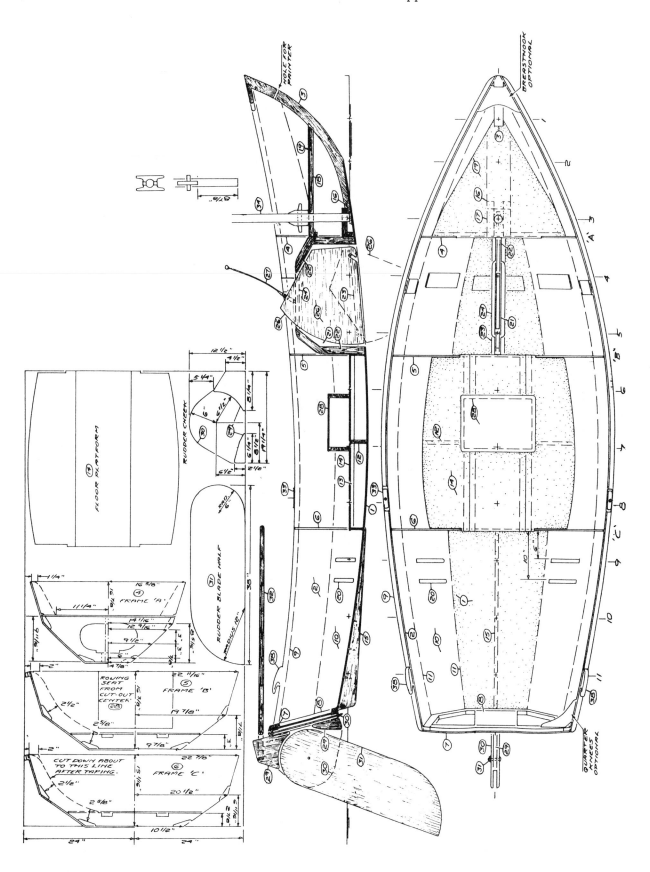

Sheet 5-3
Enlarge 250 percent for full-size plans.

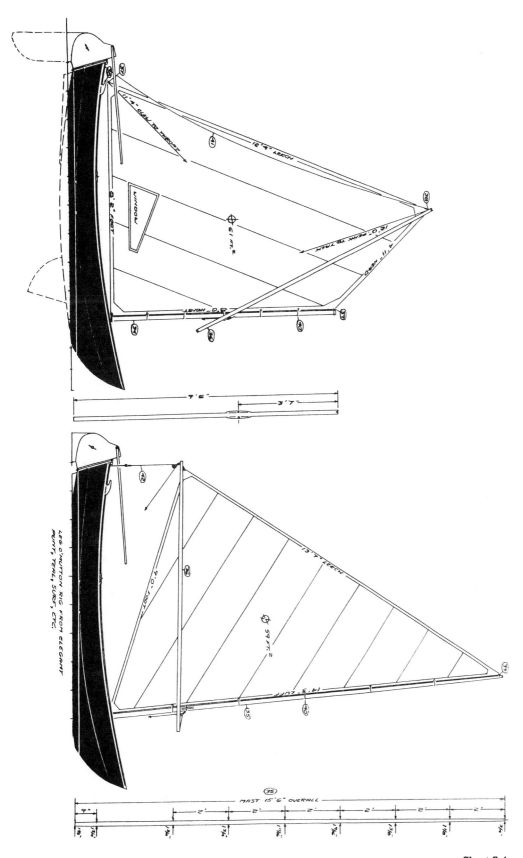

Sheet 5-4
Enlarge 500 percent for full-size plans.

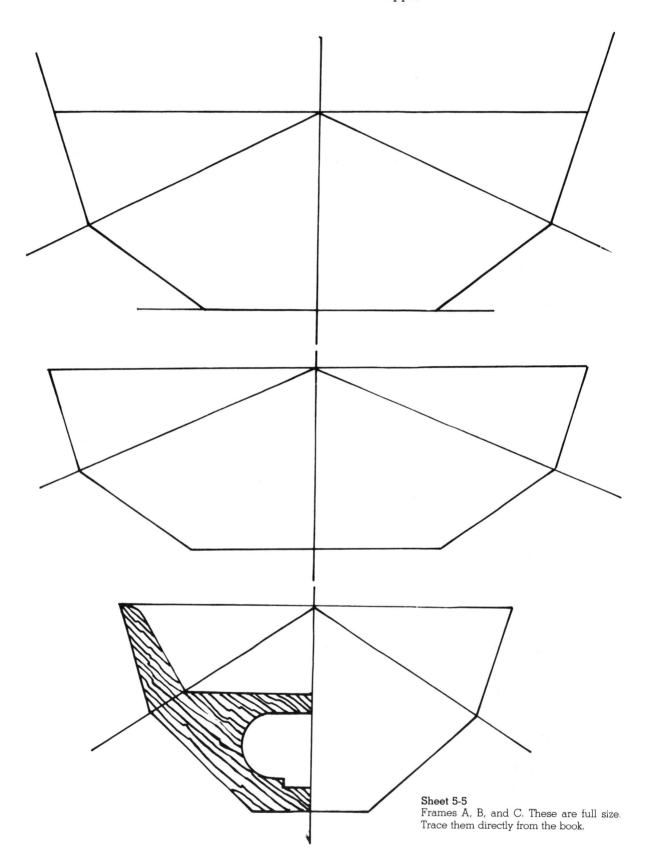

Sheet 5-5
Frames A, B, and C. These are full size.
Trace them directly from the book.

Mark the locations for frames A, B, and C on the panel (shown as dashed lines on the body plan, Sheet 5-2). Ignore the buttstraps on this as well as the other panels. Cutting pieces in half to make a butt joint called for in the full-size boat plans makes no sense—unless you plan to donate this model to a museum. We'll do this the easy way.

With the side panel all nicely traced around and frames A, B, and C located, cut out the panel with a bandsaw or scroll saw, making sure you leave the drawn line intact. Finish shaping the panel with a small plane and sandpaper. You can use the same template to draw the second side, or use the first side as a template for the second. If you use the finished side, put the two sides together and shape the second side to match the first before they go in the boat. If you don't, it will be two pencil marks wider than the first. Cut the angled ends of the panels as exactly as possible. The accuracy of the rest of the model hinges on the attention paid here.

Cut out the bottom and bilge panels next. Mark the frames and centerboard slot locations on the bottom panel. Don't bother with station marks for the bilge panels; all they do is fill space.

Cut out the transom and frame it. The frames are 1^1/$_2$ by ^{3}/$_4$ inches (^{3}/$_{16}$ x ^{3}/$_{32}$), and beveled the same on both edges. The side frames are beveled 18 degrees, bilge panels 22 degrees, and bottom 26 degrees. Leave the under edge of the top transverse frame square, and don't forget to add the ^{3}/$_4$- by 9-inch (^{3}/$_{32}$ x 1^1/$_8$) motor board.

Cut out patterns for the rudder, rudder cheek, rudder blocks, centerboard case, centerboard, foresheets, and the three frames, A, B, C. Leave the frame patterns solid (one piece), right across the top of the sheer for now.

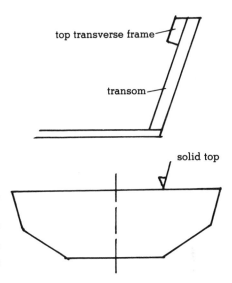

top transverse frame

transom

solid top

Let's begin by cutting or tracing a template for the stem from Sheet 5-3. Cut around the forward face of the stem, back along its straight underside, *inside* the planking, to where it nearly butts against the mast's heel (note the notch at the stem's forefoot that catches the end of the bottom panel). Cut vertically along the mast to the sheer, then along the sheer back to the stemhead. This gives you a solid piece of paper to trace around and reduces the chance of getting the stem out of whack—easily done if you tried to mark around a cutout of the skinny stem.

Lay out the stem on a piece of wood that will take its molded (profile) shape of 2^1/$_2$ inches, and its sided (plan) shape of 2 inches (^{5}/$_{16}$ x ^{1}/$_4$). After tracing the stem's forward face onto the wood, cut out its aft face from the template, reposition it on the wood, and finish tracing around it. This is the safe way to do it and guarantees getting the correct shape.

The Stem

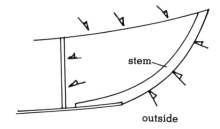

stem

outside

Try to find a piece of wood with curved grain for the stem. If you can't, move the stem template around on a straight-grain piece until the resulting cross grain is shared equally at both ends. If all the cross grain comes at one end, it's likely to break off at an inopportune time.

You can use aircraft plywood for the stem and frames if you like. Its laminated layers relieve you from having to pay attention to the grain. I didn't use plywood, myself. To me, natural wood grain is pretty and plywood isn't, so I didn't mind hunting around for a piece of wood with just the right grain. Suit yourself.

Cut out the stem and frames with a scroll saw or a jeweler's saw. Cut the ends of the stem and the notch for the mast step with your razor saw. Sand the curved face of the stem with an emery board, which bends easily to accommodate these curves, and draw a centerline on the stem's face. Rough-cut the ever-changing bevel right to the centerline, using sandpaper tacked to a block. Remember, you can always take off more wood but you can't put it back on, so make the bevel a

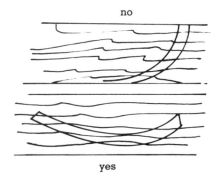

no

yes

Clockwise from upper left: Rough-cut the stem bevel with an emery board.... To guarantee accuracy, assemble the frames directly on Sheet 5-5. Work from a copy or lay wax paper over the original....True the frames' outer...and inner surfaces with an emery board.

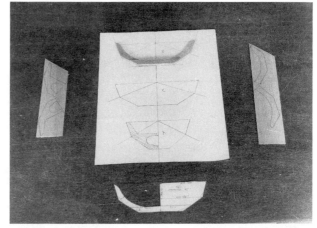
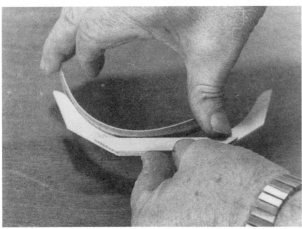
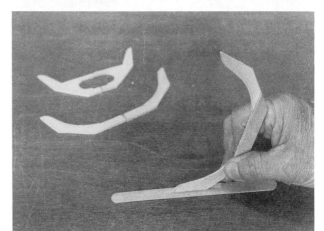

little short and fair it to its exact shape with a batten sprung around the frames before you put on the sides.

The Frames

Lay out frames A, B, and C (see Sheet 5-5) to best utilize your wood's grain pattern. If you are using straight-grained wood, move the patterns around to minimize abrupt cross grain, just as you did with the stem. To ensure accuracy, make the frames in halves, then join them together with buttstraps. Trace around the first half, then do the other, tracing around the outside of the template from the bottom centerline to the top of the frame. Cut out the frame's inside shape from the template, lay the template back on the wood, and finish tracing the frame.

Make frame A (nearest the bow) from two halves butted and strapped together, top and bottom. The top strap, across the frame's forward face above the cutout, supports the after end of the foresheets. Note that this frame has a slight curve between the edges of the bottom panel and the chine, so don't make it straight.

Make frames B and C in two halves buttstrapped together also. The buttstraps support the ends of the floor platform. The plans show notched supports for the fore-and-aft floor platform supports, but the model doesn't really need them for strength, so I left them out. I also omitted the limber holes, as I wanted the corners of the frames left intact for reference during assembly. If you want limbers in your model, make a tiny pattern for one hole and use it to mark all 12. Saw the limber hole almost free, leaving just a tiny tab (1/16 inch across is plenty) to hold it in place. You can finish cutting them out the rest of the way later. I'd use a a power scroll saw with a fine-toothed cutting blade for this job, and true up the inside and outside faces of the finished frames with an emery board.

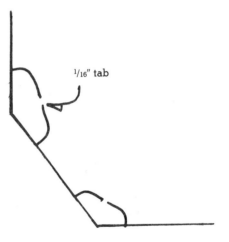

1/16" **tab**

The Centerboard and Trunk

Mark the frames' locations on the bottom panel and cut out the 3/4-inch (3/32) wide centerboard slot. Cut out both the centerboard and the trunk sides from 3/4-inch (3/32) stock, and sand both down a bit. The centerboard should be sanded thinner so it won't jam in the slot. Cut a square hole in the centerboard for the lead weight (I used a piece of chimney flashing for this), and glue the weight in place. Ordinarily, I would just paint that area grey and call it lead, but in this case doing the real thing was so easy I went for it.

Strengthen the area around the centerboard pivot pin hole with some "superglue." You can use sheet metal if you wish, but for me glue was easier. Peculiar stuff that glue. It sticks your fingers together or your eyes shut in an instant, but put a drop or two on a flat surface like this and it takes hours to

Clockwise from upper left: Frame the centerboard trunk. Drill the hole for the centerboard's pivot pin....Cut the slot in the bottom panel for the centerboard....*Cartopper's* components, laid out for assembly.

harden, even with heat to help it along. Cut the pivot pin slot in the board, using the plans as a guide, then hit the whole area with another few drops of superglue.

Frame the trunk sides with 3/4- by 1 1/2-inch (3/32 x 3/16) stock, as shown on Sheet 5-2. Hold the centerboard in place and locate the 1/2-inch (1/16) pivot-pin hole. (I used a piece of 1/16-inch brazing rod for the pivot pin.) Put the two trunk halves together and bore the hole; cut the pivot pin long enough to fit flush with the outboard edges of the trunk's sides. Cut the trunk logs 2 1/2 inches by 3/4 inch (5/16 x 3/32). This is deep enough to cover the ends of the pivot pin. Glue the trunk logs to the trunk sides, insert the pivot pin, and glue the trunk together. Put the 3/4- by 3/4-inch (3/32 x 3/32) trim around the top of the case and you are finished with it—it's ready to drop in the boat.

Hull Assembly

Start by gluing the transom to one of the sides. I used quick-grabbing Franklin Titebond here—no pins needed. Wait a few minutes until the glue sets (or you can use a small clamp hooked onto the transom's frame), then glue on the other side.

Note that the side pattern shows the forward face of frame C going on the forward dashed line, and the aft face of frame B on the aft dashed line. Put frame C (the one nearest the transom) into the boat and fasten it to the sides temporarily with pins or tape—no glue yet. Bevel frames A and B slightly by eye with a touch of sandpaper to help the sides lie in better.

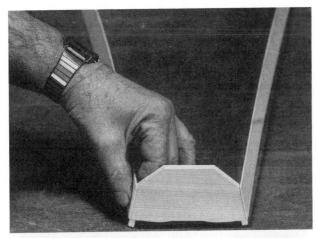

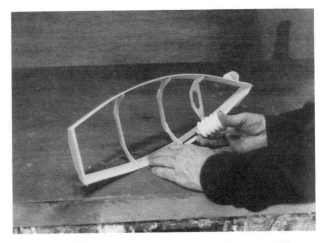

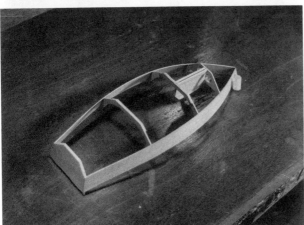

Clockwise from upper left: Begin the assembly process by gluing the sides to the transom....Tape the sides together at the bow and glue in the frames, carefully aligning the lower edges of the frames and side panels....Install the centerboard trunk now, before fitting the bottom panel.

Stick the bow ends of the sides together temporarily with masking tape (there's no stem yet), then put in frames A and B, in that order. To keep everything on one plane, align the lower (chine) edges of the sides with the chine corners of the frames (this is why we didn't cut out the limber holes). Any frames that are too high can have their tops trimmed later when you fair the top of the transom to the sides.

To save yourself a tricky fit, end-fit the centerboard trunk case between frames A and B now, before putting on the bottom panel. Pin the bottom to the transom and to frame A, and check both for alignment with the centerline. Clamp the stem to the bottom, with the forward end of the bottom panel bearing against the notch in the bottom of the stem. Bring in the sides and trial fit them to the stem. Take your time here and adjust the stem, stem notch, and bottom panel so the ends of the side panels lay fair to the rake of the stem. When you're satisfied all is well, spread glue on one side of the stem, and

Clockwise from upper left: Pin the bottom panel in place temporarily and trial fit the stem. When everything looks fair, glue the side panels in place.... Glue the bottom panel in place....Align the centerboard trunk with the centerboard slot by using two scraps of wood....Hold the bilge panels with masking tape during the sand-and-fit stage; bisect the panels with a relocating mark.

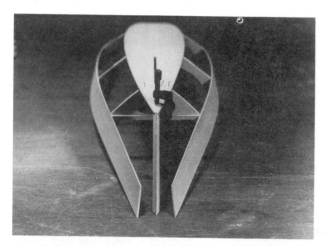

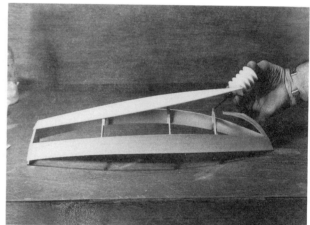

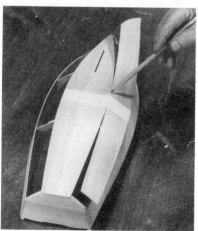

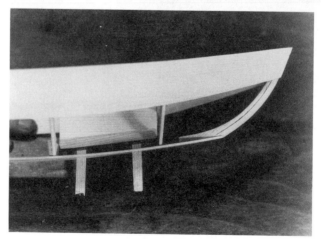

hold or pin the plank in place until the glue sets. Repeat the process for the other side.

Take off the bottom panel and spread glue on all the frame bottoms, the transom framing, and the section of the stem on which the bottom lands. Put the bottom back on, carefully aligning the stem and frames with the bottom's centerline. Stick a couple pieces of 3/4-inch (3/32) scrap in the centerboard case slot for guides; spread glue on the ends of the trunk and the trunk logs, and slip the case in place (take out the guides before the glue hardens).

Fitting The Bilge Panels

She's really shaping up now. To finish the hull, all we need do is close her in with the bilge panels. Locate their fore-and-aft position on the boat, leaving some overhang at the ends. If the panels seem too stiff forward, taper them a bit with sandpaper; you won't need to wet them to make the bend. Draw a relocating line across the bilge and bottom panel joint, just as we did with *Bobcat.* Each time you take off the bilge panel for fitting, place it back on this mark. Hold the panel in place temporarily with a piece of masking tape while you fit it.

It's easy to make a mistake here. Fit the middle of the panel first, then keep working toward the ends. Cut the panels slightly oversize, tape them to the outside of the hull, and mark their shape from inside, using the edges of the sides and bottom panel as guides. Don't assume that you can use one perfectly fitting panel as a pattern for the other; fit both individually. Think of an orange section as you fit these panels together, taking a little off the inside edges of the bottom panel, the side panel, and the bilge panel. Sand and fit, sand and fit, until they fit like a glove.

When you're satisfied with the fit of both panels (don't forget to mark them to distinguish between port and starboard), spread glue on all the bearing surfaces and put the panels on, one at a time. Don't try to rush the job and do both at once; you may have to face the embarrassing realization that you glued the wrong side to the boat. Just one guess why I know that!

Start in the middle of the panel and bring both ends together at the stem and stern. Because Titebond glue grabs so quickly (especially with high temperature and low humidity), you might find the edges of the panel sticking before you have it steered into place, or the edges might stick before they are aligned exactly fore-and-aft. To get around this, I'd use regular Elmer's white glue everywhere between the transom and stem, and save the quick-grabbing glue for the ends. Those are the last to stick down and the easiest to align. Hold the side panel in place while the glue dries with a couple of pins toe-nailed to its top edge. After it dries, cut and sand the ends of the bilge panels and the rest of the planking flush with the transom. Don't round the corners; leave them sharp.

Fitting Out the Interior

Make the mast step from a scrap of wood $1/2$ inch by $6^{1/4}$ by 5 inches ($1/16$ x $3/4$ x $5/8$), and mark a centerline on it. With a small bevel gauge, take the rake for the rig you've chosen from Sheet 5-4, and use the gauge as a guide for cutting the hole for the heel of the mast. For the sprit rig, bore a round, $1^{5/8}$-inch ($21/32$) hole; make a 2-inch ($1/4$) square hole for the leg-o'-mutton rig. Now glue the mast step in place.

Cut out the floor platform pattern from Sheet 5-3, and make the platform from three edge-glued strips of $3/4$-inch ($3/32$) thick by 1-foot ($1^{1/2}''$) wide wood. Fit this in place in the boat, but don't glue it; it is supposed to be removable. The model won't need the extra floor platform reinforcement shown on the plans, but you can add it if you're a stickler for details.

The bow seat, or foresheets, is one of the trickiest fits in the boat—sort of like making a breast hook, the easily bungled shape of which has fed many a fire—including my own. If you can make it fit all at one crack, chalk one up for you. I spent an hour or so making mine, had a nice fit everywhere, then blew it by cutting the mast hole without double-checking my rule. Murphy seemed pleased.

Cut out a template for the foresheets, which we'll make from two pieces of $1^{3/4}$-inch or wider stock edge-glued together. Allow a good $1/4$ inch extra for the template on the aft part of the seat—which misses its fit to the inboard edges of frame A by quite a bit, and along the edges. These appear straight in the plans, but actually are curved—one of those

Glue the mast step to the aft end of the stem and the forward face of Frame A, then fit the foresheets—a tricky job.

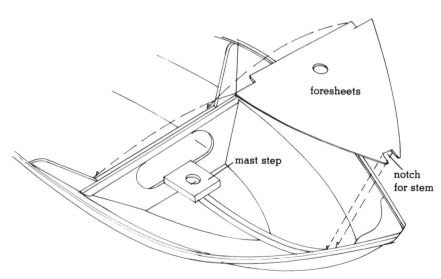

foresheets

mast step

notch for stem

optical illusions which make boatbuilding interesting. Lay the seat template on the wood you are using and trace its shape; allow plenty of wood to work with outside your template. Try the foresheets in the hull and fit it everywhere, then install the mast partner underneath (just a scrap of wood to stiffen the deck here) and bore a hole for the mast. I didn't glue the foresheets in place because I wanted to be able to pick it out to show the mast step and stem detail to prospective builders.

The movable rowing seat is a plain box measuring 5 inches by 1 foot by 1 foot 4 inches ($5/8$ x $1^1/2$ x 2), easily built with your planer-blade equipped table saw if it has an accurate miter gauge.

Now that we've done the hard part, we're left with all the goodies that elevate this little craft to mantelpiece status: the gunwales, the rudder, the skeg, the waterline, and the mast, sprit, and sail.

Sand the bow face of the hull planking straight across; if you rock your sanding block you won't get a good joint for your stemcap. Cut a $1/2$ by about 2-inch strip of wood—wide enough to overlap whatever you've used for planking, and long enough plus a little more to span the length from stem-head to bottom panel. Saw this out square-edged, making no attempt to taper or shape it to match the sides (we'll do that later). For now just fit it nicely to the face of the stem. Wet the outside of the bend with your tongue and prebend it with your fingers to the approximate curve; glue it in place, holding it temporarily with pins.

While you're waiting for the glued stemcap to set up, rip out the gunwales. These can be 1 inch by $3/4$ inch ($1/8$ x $3/32$), rather than the double $1/2$-inch gunwales called for in the plans. For more contrast saw these and the stemcap from a fine-grained, darker wood. I had none on hand, so I made both the gunwales and stemcap from birch soaked overnight in household ammonia, which turns light-colored wood a pretty coffee color. You won't need a tank: just wrap the wood strips in a paper towel and pour ammonia over them, then wrap the whole works in waxed paper and let it set a few hours or overnight. If the strips dry out too much they will harden, but just soak them a bit more—or hit their outside edge with your tongue—and they'll bend in fine.

After the glue on the stemcap dries, work it down fair to the sides, bilge panel, and bottom. This gives a precision fit without having to be precise, and avoids the chance of gluing a nicely fitted stem askew.

The gunwales go on next. Spread glue as evenly as you can on one, clamp it at the bow with one clamp, and feed it along the sheer, pressing it against the planking with your

Stemcap and Gunwales

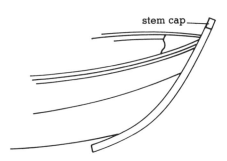

Glue on square-edged strip of wood to cover stem area. Fair to hull after glue dries.

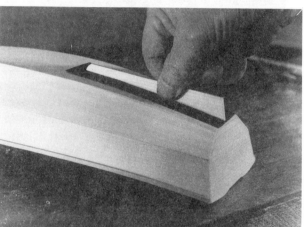

fingers as you go. You'll need a couple of clamps near the transom because of the quick hook in her sheer.

Trim the ends of the gunwales, then lay the transom template on the inside of the transom. Align the top corners of the template with those of the transom, mark its shape, then trim it to the proper contour. Cut off the ends of the transom framing and fair them down to the gunwales.

Cut out the skeg template along the edge next to the hull, leaving extra paper beneath the skeg so the template won't edge-set. Mark the hull edge of the skeg on a piece of 3/4-inch (3/32) wood, then finish cutting out the rest of the skeg template. Put this back on the wood and finish tracing, then cut out the skeg. Lay a piece of sandpaper on the hull's bottom panel and rub the skeg side to side until it hunkers down for a tight fit, then glue it on.

Cut out templates for the rudder's parts: one rudder blade, one rudder cheek, and the 3/4-inch (3/32) thick filler blocks shown on Sheet 5-3. Cut out the parts from 1/16-inch thick

Clockwise from upper left: Glue on the stem cap, leaving plenty of extra material. Work it down fair with the hull later....Glue on the gunwales; trim their ends with a razor saw held parallel to the sides....Lay sandpaper in the way of the skeg and rub it around until it fits perfectly....Cut out and assemble the rudder's parts; drill the pivot hole.

Skeg and Rudder

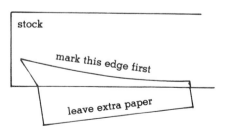

stock

mark this edge first

leave extra paper

wood, and glue the filler blocks in place on the rudder cheek. Fair off the rudder on its leading and trailing edges.

We want this rudder to pivot up for shallow water. You'll need a small machine screw and a wingnut to hold the rudder to the rudder cheek. Finding the machine screw is no problem, but finding a wingnut this small is another matter. The easiest course is to mold one from epoxy or polyester resin. Make a template from the wingnut pattern, lay it on a scrap of thin wood, drill three equidistant holes, and cut the wingnut's shape between them. Wax the elementary mold you've made and lay it on a sheet of waxed paper. Plop in a nut that fits your machine screw, pour the resin around it, let it harden, and you've got a wingnut. You might as well make two while you're at it. If you cut the head off the machine screw and replace it with your homemade wingnuts, you can hold one while tightening the other.

If you aspire to metalsmithery, and if you have a small tap-and-die set, you can make a wingnut from sheet brass. Trace the wingnut's shape on brass about 1/8-inch thick, cut it out with a fine-tooth jeweler's saw, and file it to shape. Now drill and tap the hole for the machine screw.

While you're in the metal fabrication business, you might as well make the gudgeons and pintles. The easy way out is to use common pins bent to shape. But since you've just become an experienced metalsmith, consider making them from hobby shop sheet brass, copper flashing—whatever is thin, workable, and available.

I cut out all this rudder and tiller hardware with my bandsaw, using the back of a handsaw clamped to the table for a guide. Sawing this thin sheet metal is tricky. The saw teeth catch the metal's edge and distort it to junk if you feed it too fast or saw it unsupported over the blade's slot. Best to run a scrap board into the blade first and use that as a sawing platform. Saw out a metal strip the width you need, then cut the individual pieces to length with an old razor saw blade. It's a good idea to save your old saw blades for just such a job as this.

For the gudgeons and pintles, cut a 5/32-inch wide strip of sheet metal, then cut four pieces the same length, about 9/32 inch. Put them in your vise and bend a right angle in them, then round their ends with a file. Clamp two of them together over a scrap of 1/8-inch thick wood (this represents the clearance between the rudder and the transom) and bore a small hole about the size of the 18-gauge escutcheon pin (a number 55 twist drill is close) we'll use for the rudder's pivot pin. Glue the gudgeons to the transom and rudder cheek blocks with Titebond glue. While this dries, we can make *Cartopper's* tiller.

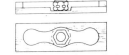

Wingnut Pattern (actual size)

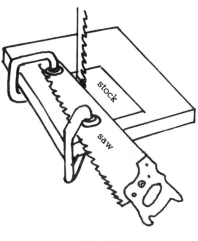

Rudder Brackets (actual size)

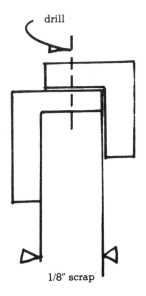

drill

1/8" scrap

The tiller is 3 feet 8 inches (5½ inches) long, tapered forward of the rudderhead from 2 inches to 1¾ inches (¼ to 7/32). Cut the two 1- by 10-inch (⅛ x 1¼) straps that secure the tiller to the rudder from sheet brass or from whatever's thin and handy.

Clamp the two straps together on a scrap board and measure the locations of the holes from the plans. Prick punch the centers of the holes with a very sharp awl, then bore the holes for the pins. Boring these tiny holes by hand takes a good eye and steady hands. Save making miniature hardware like this for whatever part of the day you work best and shake less. My friend Jim Betts, who did the ever-popular *Understanding Boat Design* with Ted Brewer, had a saying about modelmaking in general that fits this job in particular: "By the time I drink enough to keep my hands from shaking, I don't see so well."

At any rate, glue the straps to the tiller, let them dry, then bore for the pins from both directions, hoping to meet in the middle. Don't try to bore by hand from one side only, trying to hit the hole on the other side. You aren't likely to do it.

The Tiller

Clockwise from upper left: Glue the predrilled rudder straps to the tiller and bore for the pin hole from both sides, meeting in the middle....Peen a head on the brass pins, locking the rudder straps to the tiller....Mount the tiller on the rudderhead with peened over brass pins, too; leave a little slack so the tiller will pivot upward. Note the cast-resin wingnut.

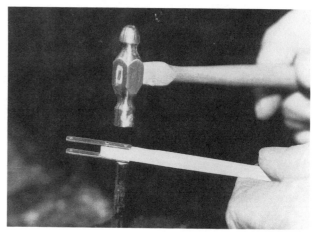

Now put a brass pin in your vise and head it over with a modeler's ball peen hammer; slip the pin through the tiller strap and cut off the excess with the razor saw, allowing a little extra length for peening. Rest the pin's first peened end on a machinists' punch (or something else hard) held in your vise, and peen over the other end. Now do the second pin and alternate whacking them so they tighten together.

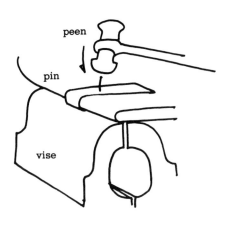

Slip the strap end of the tiller over the head of the rudder cheek block and try the tiller for position; allow enough clearance between the end of the tiller and cheek block so the tiller is free to come to about horizontal at rest. When you're satisfied with the location, bore for the pin—just the way you did on the tiller—insert it, and peen it over as tight as you want. Leave enough slack so the tiller can pivot up out of the way.

Raising the Centerboard; Belaying the Sheets; Bracing Your Feet

Now we can raise our rudder when we want our model to go aground; you'll want to do the same thing with your centerboard. You could just bore a hole through the centerboard and put a string through it, but there's a neater and more challenging way. Make straps to hold the centerboard pendant from the same brass sheet as the tiller straps (take the dimensions from Sheet 5-2). Put the straps in your vise, round the top a bit with a file, and bore a hole in the top for the pendant pin. Cut or file a notch to hold the pendant strap in each side of the centerboard at the spot shown in the plans, and glue the strap in place. If it is a little thicker than the board, file or sand it flush.

Make the pendant from the same 1/16-inch brazing rod (or other similar material) as the centerboard pivot pin. Cut the pendant wire to length and flatten one end with a hammer until it fits in the slot between the straps. Bore a hole in it, pin it through the strap, and peen the ends. After varnishing or painting the centerboard, feed it up into the trunk, hooking the pivot pin slot over the pin. Stick the pendant up through the trunk and glue a wooden knob, a glass bead—whatever appeals—to the pendant's end to keep it from falling through the centerboard slot.

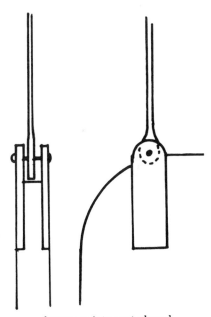

let straps into centerboard

If your shop is no neater than mine, drop one of these small parts and it's gone forever. My paint-spattered shop floor is no help either; small parts like that are eaten like snacks. As a precaution, I lay parts out on a piece of paper, and if I'm working with something in a vise I set a bucket under it—not that a dropped part won't hit the bucket's rim and go flying, which always pleases Mr. Murphy.

The sheet hooks—made from a few scraps of wood glued to the gunwale at the spot shown in Sheet 5-3—are designed to keep even the dumbest of us out of trouble. You'd really

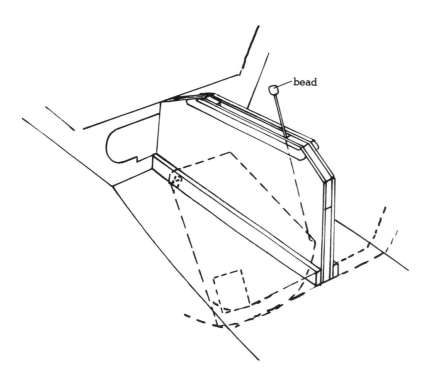
bead

Glue a bead to the end of the centerboard pennant to keep it from falling back into the trunk.

have to work at it to get a couple of hitches of your sheet to stay long enough around that tapered thumb to flip you over. But after hearing from a builder who has them on another, similar boat who managed to do it, and got his can wet in the process, I've learned never to underestimate the ingenuity of some poor souls hell-bent on their own self-destruction.

Cut a template from the plans, trace the sheet hooks' shape onto a scrap of wood, and cut them out. Put them together and work on them paired so they will come out alike. Round them well with an emery board; round their inside edges with a small round file.

Make four foot stretchers from 3/4-inch (3/32) square stock, about 7 inches (7/8) long. Measure their location in the boat, and space them out with a scrap of wood as you glue them down. They don't have to be off much to look sloppy, and one out of line gets noticed right off quick.

Scribing the Waterline and Finishing

We've gotten this far; it's time to think about the finishing process. Will you use paint or varnish? I definitely went for varnish and for two reasons: it's the easiest to apply and I like looking at wood grain.

Before striking the waterline, we need to seal the hull so the pencil won't catch the grain and run off. Handle the model as little as possible until it's covered with a sealing coat of thinned paint or varnish. (You might consider getting some

cheap, thin cotton gloves if you can't leave it alone.) Check it over carefully, and do any necessary sanding with 320-grit or finer paper. I varnished *Cartopper's* pieces first, before doing the hull, so I could see how I liked what I stirred up with my homebrew varnish. Lay out all the parts and coat everything with one or two *thin* coats, sanding in between.

With the hull sealed we're ready to strike the waterline, and we'll do it the simple way: Set the model on a flat surface and scribe the waterline around, using a pencil held on a block of wood equal to the waterline's height.

Cartopper's body plan (Sheet 5-2) shows a boottop and a LWL (load waterline). Mark the boottop first. Measure from the top of the boot to her bottom amidships at her greatest depth—7 inches (7/8 inch; you are using 1½-inch scale, right?). Cut a block of wood that thick by 1½ inches wide by 3 or 4 inches long.

Set the model on a flat surface and raise the stern up or down until the top of the block of wood matches the height of the boot top at the extreme aft end. Weight the model down so it won't skitter around, and with the sharp point of an awl or pencil, scribe the boottop around.

Now let's shift gears, or in this case, scales. Lay your scale rule on the boottop of the sail plan (3/4-inch scale). The scale rule says the boottop is ½-inch wide, so take ½ inch (1/16 inch—take off a slice with your table saw) off the block and go around again. Measure again from the underside of the boottop to the top of the LWL—2½ inches (5/16). Slice that much off the block, go around once more, and that does it. Use a light touch with the pencil or awl. As I said, this method is very simple, but you do have to stop and think. And it sure helps to let a scale rule do much of the thinking for you.

Left to right: This is a good time to finish all the parts. Note the foot stretchers and the sheet hooks, just fore and aft, respectively, of my varnish brush...Scribing the waterline.

Mast, Sprit, and Sail

The spritsail is one of my favorite rigs for a number of reasons, the first being that it is very forgiving for the novice sailor. Unlike a boomed sail, which doesn't mind knocking your head off if you forget to duck during a surprise jibe, the spritsail's loose foot brushes harmlessly over your head. If you are on a run and suddenly realize that you might be overpowered by wind that piped up unnoticed, the rotating mast allows you to let the sheet go, cover your eyes, and let the boat take care of herself as the sail—sheet and all—blows out ahead. This saved my neck a number of times when I was first learning to sail.

As simple as this rig is, I'm often asked how it works on the full-size boat. To set the sail, catch the *pigtail* tied into the top grommet at the peak of the sail in the sprit slot, and catch the knotted end of the *snotter* in the slot at the other end of the sprit. Reeve the snotter up through the eye of the *sling* and push up on the heel of the sprit with the palm of your hand while pulling down on the snotter. This drives the peak of the sail up taut. Keep tension on the snotter and make it fast to the cleat. The leg-o'-mutton rig works exactly the same way, but the sprit boom is horizontal.

If you're wondering what all this real-boat talk has to do with a model, refer back to the preface. Boat modeling has little to do with reality. Besides, you may want to build one of these full size some day. Far better to learn to rig a sprit snotter in the privacy of your workshop at $1^{1}/_{2}$-inch scale than with a kibitzing audience of piling perchers and other waterfront undesirables cheering your efforts.

The mast and sprit are both 9 feet 6 inches ($14^{1}/_{4}$ inches) long, and are most easily made from a $^{1}/_{4}$-inch dowel. If you like, taper the sprit a little at the peak, starting about 3 or 4 feet ($4^{1}/_{2}$ to 6 inches) from the end. Taper the heel a little less than the peak, starting about $2^{1}/_{2}$ feet ($3^{3}/_{4}$ inches) from the bottom end. Taper both sprit and mast to whatever suits your eye; I didn't bother to taper mine at all. Notch both ends of the sprit to catch the sail's pigtail at the peak and the snotter at the heel.

The mast has two 1- by 10-inch ($^{1}/_{16}$ or so by $1^{1}/_{4}$) cleats to hold the rope sling. To find their center, measure 3 feet 7 inches ($5^{3}/_{8}$ inches) down from the masthead. Using a miniature needle file, file a groove $^{1}/_{16}$-inch deep in each cleat and glue them to the mast. Make another cleat, similar to the one shown on the mast in Sheet 5-3, and glue it to the forward face of the mast just above the foresheets. This is where we'll belay the snotter. Slot the top of the mast to receive the sail's throat lashing.

Speaking of sails, this is a good time to think about making one. Few things spoil the looks of a model more than a poorly made sail. I wouldn't try to stitch one myself—not after watching one of the best seamstresses around fail to do it. And I

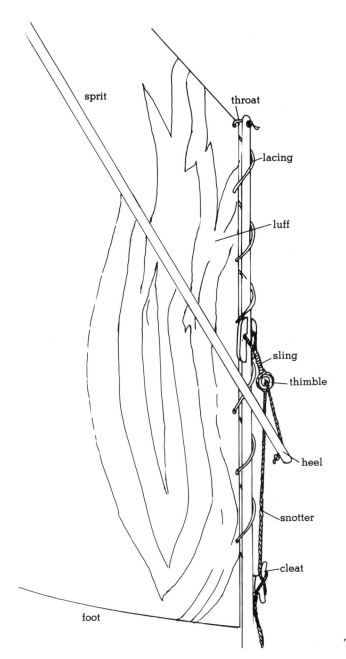

sprit

throat

lacing

luff

sling

thimble

heel

snotter

cleat

foot

The sprit rig revealed.

wanted the sail to look right for this model even if I had to make it from green cheese—no wrinkles, no droops allowed. What I finally came up with is a sheet of ¹/₃₂-inch birch plywood—curled just the way I wanted it. I've never been pleased with warped wood before, but this one caught my eye and said, "SAIL!"

Look at the sail plan (Sheet 5-4) and note that the *luff* (that's the edge of the sail along the mast) looks square to the *foot* (bottom edge). It may *look* square, but it isn't. Lay your square against the luff with the arm of the square touching the *clew*

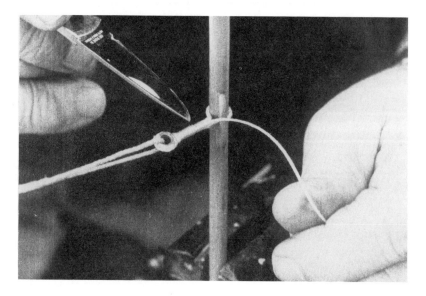

Glue and seize the sling between the mast and thimble. Trim the end of the seizing twine flush.

(extreme aft end) and you will see that it's 2 inches (¼) out of square at the *tack* (forward lower corner). Using your square, first draw a right angle, then draw a line representing the sail's foot 8 feet 2 inches (12¼ inches) long, the length from tack to clew. (Your 12-inch piece of aircraft plywood is ¼ inch too short, so you'll need to cut off a piece from the corner of the sheet and edge-glue it on to make up the difference.) Add 2 inches (¼ inch) vertically below the line at the tack; connect the tack and clew with a straight line, and you have established the starting point that controls the shape of the rest of the sail. All you have to do now is measure 8 feet (12 inches) along the luff, 4 feet 11 inches (7⅜ inches) along the head, and 12 feet 4 inches (18½ inches) along the *leech* (the after edge). Connect these points and there's the shape of your sail. Cut it out, give it a sealer coat of varnish, bore holes for the sail ties—one each at the peak, throat, clew, tack, and five spaced evenly along the luff—and you're in business.

You'll need some thin twine to bend the sail to the mast, plus some for the sling, snotter, sail ties, and sheet. I found a piece of three-strand nylon kite string, about 1/32-inch diameter, which worked nicely for everything.

My fingers just couldn't splice this small stuff I used to make the sling, so I made a continuous loop around the mast, keeping it as short as possible, and seized it with smaller nylon after the thimble was in. The snotter runs through the thimble as you tighten the sprit or spritboom. A rope eye will work, but nowhere near as easily as a nice, smooth brass thimble.

"Where will I find a thimble this size?" you say. The brass screw cap from a spark plug provided mine—it even came bored and with lines around it to serve as a guide for slicing off what I wanted. Like any thimble, it needs a groove around it to

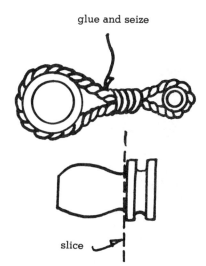

glue and seize

slice

hold the twine, so put the cap in your vise with its ends bearing against the jaws, and file a groove with a small, round needle file. Slice off what you need with a razor saw, pinch the sling together with a bit of glue, and seize it with a small piece of $1/64$-inch diameter nylon.

I used a simple seizing I learned as a Sea Scout. Take a length of the seizing twine, lay one end lengthwise along the sling—about halfway between the thimble and the mast—and wrap tightly along it to just past the halfway point. Hold your tight wraps in place, and wrap right along, this time loosely, to the mast. Now take the free end of the twine, feed it back through the loose wraps, and snug each wrap down while pulling on the free end. When they're all lying fair and tight, haul the free end taut and cut it off flush. No knots—it's all done in one continuous piece. Give it a coat of varnish or glue and it looks right professional.

Now it's time to bend the sail to the mast. Bore a small fore-and-aft hole—just large enough to pass your lacing twine—as close to the masthead as you dare (if it's too close to the end, you might split the mast). Reeve the lacing through the hole from the forward face of the mast; tie a knot in the end to keep it from slipping through, and let it stand proud. Start at

If you really get carried away, paint the sail—off-white or tanbark—and draw in the lines of stitching parallel to the leech a scale 32 inches apart. Me? I'd rather see the wood grain—even if it is plywood.

the top grommet (the holes you bored in the sail) at the throat and lace the sail along the luff to the rest of the grommets. Phil says "separate ties," not lacing. If one grommet tie lets go you keep on sailing; if a lacing lets go, the whole thing comes down. I couldn't face tying that many knots, however, so I went the lacing route. Besides, models are seldom caught on a lee shore with their sails down.

Tie in a pigtail (just a simple loop and overhand knot) at the peak grommet of the sail, leaving it about 1/4 inch higher than the peak. Make it just long enough so that it sits in the sprit slot with a little slop. Set the sprit up taut and she's all rigged.

In the Cradle

After this much work, you'll want to show off *Cartopper* properly, so let's make her a cradle. First make a base, about 1/8 or 3/16 inch thick by 4 1/2 by 7 inches, from the wood of your choice. I didn't have anything that wide on hand, so I edge-glued together three pieces of cedar planking.

Place frame templates B and C on a piece of wood about 3/16 inch by 1 1/8 inch by 9 inches, and trace their shape, allowing for the thickness of the planking. Measure the distance between the frames on the plans, then glue the pieces to the base that distance apart. Give the cradle a coat or two of varnish, and *Cartopper's* finished.

The Peapod

Win Some, Lose Some,
Learn Some

Peapods and double-enders have always fascinated me. I got my first lesson in seamanship aboard one, at the tender age of 12 or 13, and almost drowned in the process. Fishermen along our rockbound Maine Coast all said that a peapod or double-ender was the most seaworthy boat I could possibly find—the one they'd pick if they had to ride out a gale. "Lay right down in the bottom of her," they said, "and she'll ride out anything."

As teenage boys are wont to do, I listened to the first part, but the second part—about keeping your weight low—went right past me. "What the hell, it's the most seaworthy boat in the world. I won't need any brains to go with it," said my wonderful, see-everything-in-black-and-white teenage brain. So when I borrowed a lobsterman's peapod one fall day to bring in the rest of my lobster pots (my old dory had packed it in), I loaded her up with heavy, soaked traps, stacked nice and high across the gunwales, and I didn't bother to tie them down. It was getting cold and I wanted them to be easy to unload.

I didn't need to worry about unloading them. About halfway in from the spindle ledge to the beach in Rockland the 'pod fetched a roll and my pots slid over the side. I never looked back; just rowed like hell for shore—plenty shaken, but thanking my lucky stars that I had been too lazy to tie the pots down. If I had, I would have gone bottom-up for sure. It was a good lesson. I learned that a seaworthy boat isn't that seaworthy if it has a brainless skipper.

Years later I lobstered out of a peapod on Metinic Island—about eight miles northeast of Monhegan. By now I knew enough to pile the traps in the *bottom* of the boat and go easy with the top load. What a delight it was rowing that 'pod—standing up, facing forward, right in around the rocks and through the breakers. Her fine ends enabled me to back out of tight spots that would put a square-stern boat on the beach, pushed sideways by a following sea.

But no matter how nice it was, fishing out of a peapod couldn't last forever. I used to come in from hauling with one crate of lobsters, but my neighbor, who had just steamed by me in his powerboat—motor roaring, radio blasting, and power winch turning like crazy—would have five crates. By the time I got back in, he'd be sitting in his island camp sipping a cool one with his feet up and his slippers on, watching me struggle toward my mooring under oars.

With economic reality staring me in the face, I joined the race, bought a powerboat, and forgot all about double-enders and peapods, until one day I visited the shipmodel section of the Farnsworth Museum in Rockland, Maine. There sat the most exquisite model of a peapod I ever laid eyes on: carvel planked, all properly spiled and hollowed over steam-bent timbers (you could even see the tiny fastenings). It had everything: breasthooks, floorboards, right on down to the oarlocks and oars—perfect in every way. The tag said it was made by Elmer Montgomery. Now that surprised me. I happened to know Elmer, and knew he never worked a day in a boatyard in

So what's the difference between a peapod and a double-ender? Well, not much. They differed more by locale than by appearance. Double-enders usually had both ends alike. Peapods varied considerably, with the bow section often being higher and finer than the stern. Both could be flat or round bottom, and have stiff or slack bilges according to the owner's whims—what they thought made a good rowing or workboat. Peapods and double-enders with more deadrise and softer bilges both planked and rowed more easily. A flatter bottom meant the boat was harder to plank and slower to row.

My own choice for a workboat was either a double-ender or a peapod with a flatter-than-normal bottom, which made it easier to stand in and work from all day without slipping and sliding around. Also, tubs of bait stowed better in the flatter-bottomed boat. Just tip over a tub of greasy herring cuttings in a round-bottomed boat, then try standing up in it the rest of the day, hauling traps over the side in a slop! My first priority was comfortable working conditions; rowing was second. As long as the boat had reasonably fine ends (I liked some hollow to the waterline), the flatter the bottom the better.

his life. In fact he was a banker, and had been president of the Rockland Savings and Loan for years.

How does someone who claims not to be a boatbuilder turn out something as nice as that model? Well, being curious, I asked. Elmer said he built it in 1937 when he was 26 years old, from plans he drew himself to his own design. He used to hang around Snow's Shipyard here in Rockland when he was a high school kid, and in particular around resident designer Albert Congdon, who also designed draggers for Newbert and Wallace, the famed boatbuilders of Thomaston, Maine. "Albert was good to me," Elmer said. "He never lost patience, and he answered every question I had."

Elmer Montgomery and his inspirational peapod.

Elmer built a couple of full-size 15-footers, but never pursued boatbuilding as a profession. When I asked him why, he said that his real interest was models—not full-size boats, and he didn't think he could make a living building models back during the Great Depression. Instead, he worked as a messenger for a Rockland bank for $10.00 a week, and spent his evenings and weekends building this model—all with hand tools.

Years later I found myself in the boatbuilding business, with plans for a Phil Bolger-designed peapod in hand. I had lofted the boat full size, but to make my initial mistakes more affordable I thought I should make a model first. Not being shy about benefiting from another's experience, I went looking for Elmer, to ask him what kind of problems I might run into.

Now ordinarily, carvel-planked boats are built over temporary molds that are ribbanded, then timbered and planked. But not Elmer's carvel-planked model. He built it upside down, as the real boats often were, but then planked it without first using ribbands or timbering—totally opposite from the time-honored practice. He put in the timbers after planking, the same as you do in strip planking. This was the first time I had heard of doing it this way and it appealed to me. I could get right to the fun of planking and skip the tedious timbering and ribbanding part. But it also meant lining off and spiling the planks very carefully or they wouldn't hang right. I understood all this, but I didn't know whether I actually could do it—especially not in miniature, where so many of the physical rules that govern full-size boatbuilding just don't seem to apply.

As it turned out I couldn't. Ever-watchful Murphy won this one and seemed pleased. When I got to the turn of the bilge, the planking started to lay off the molds in a most unpleasing fashion. I gave up, accepted defeat as graciously as I could, and tried to figure out the whys and whats for a later attempt.

I tried carvel planking this hard-bilged peapod later, going back to the conventional way of doing it. I got her all timbered and ribbanded, with the planking nicely lined off, but the thought of shaping and hollowing all those planks discouraged me. (I'll show you how to get that far at the end of this chapter; if you want to go ahead and plank her, try Robert Steward's *Boatbuilding Manual* {IMP, 1987}, or Richard Mansir's *A Modeler's Guide to Hull Construction* {TAB Books, 1984}. Either one should allow you to finish carvel planking her.) Then it came to me to build her the easy way: strip planks. I'll show you how to do this simple and elegant method—which you can apply to any round-bottom boat. Then we'll make oars, oarlocks—the works.

Materials Needed:

- 1/2-inch plywood, about 2 by 2 feet
- fine-grained hardwood, 3/16 by 2 inches by about 16 inches
- straight-grained softwood, 1 by 4 or 5 inches by about 26 inches

Tools Needed:

- the standard tool kit, plus . . .
- a sharp planer blade for your table saw
- a good pair of dividers
- Payson's Patent Glue Spreader (read on)
- pincurlers

The Plans

This peapod is 15 feet long with a 4-foot beam; she has either a sailing or rowing keel; her sections are quite flat with stiff bilges, particularly at station 3. The stem and sternpost, whether laminated or double-sawn, land on either the sailing keel or on a 1 1/2-inch square rowing keel. Her frames and floor timbers are 5/8 inch by 1 1/4 inches, steam-bent or laminated, spaced on 6-inch centers. The carvel planking is 3/8-inch thick, ten or eleven strakes per side; the wales are 5/8-inch plank. She has 3/4-inch by 1 1/2-inch stemcaps, bent or laminated, that are put on after she's planked. Her plans (Sheet 6-1) were drawn originally to the scale of 1 inch equals 1 foot, and came with a table of offsets and an ample supply of buttock lines and water-lines to ensure lofting a reasonably accurate hull.

But, to me, this 1-inch-to-the-foot scale is too small, and thus less forgiving of clumsy fingers, dull pencils, and poor eyesight. Besides, larger models are more fun to play with, so I scaled it up to 1 1/2 inches to the foot.

It Can't Be This Easy

After the previous models in this book—chine boats, easily built from measurements—building a round-bottom boat like this one might seem like alchemy, but not to worry. I've drawn all the molds and the bow and stern patterns full-size (Sheets 6-3 and 6-4). Just trace the molds directly from the book, cut them out (mark the sheer lines and the approximate location of the starter plank on the edges of the molds), mount them on 1/4-inch plywood or the like with 3M Spra-ment or any non-waterbased glue, and saw them out on your bandsaw or with a sabersaw.

Now make a building base from a piece of 1/2-inch thick plywood, 6 inches wide by 2 feet long. If you have access to a big photocopier (check your Yellow Pages for "Blue Printing"), have Sheet 6-2 enlarged to full size, glue it right to the base, and you're ready to glue down the mold stations and build away.

If you can't find a photocopying service, or if it's snowing or a holiday and you don't want to wait, take the same piece of ½-inch plywood for the building base, but make sure that one side and one end have the factory-cut edges, which are reliably square. Draw a centerline on the board, measuring its location accurately from the *factory-cut edge*. Now, hook a two-foot rule over the factory-cut end, and, starting with the F.P. (Forward Perpendicular), make a tick mark on the centerline as you transfer the measurements for each mold station. *Don't move your rule as you do this!* You'll build in a cumulative measuring error that will make for one peculiar-looking boat.

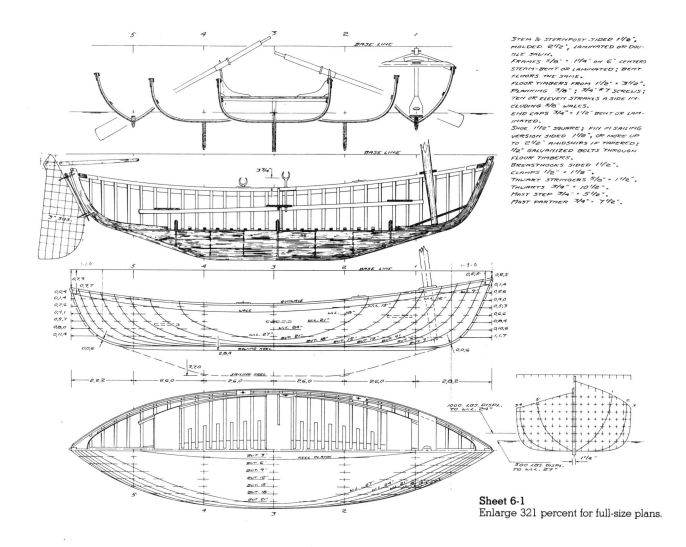

Sheet 6-1
Enlarge 321 percent for full-size plans.

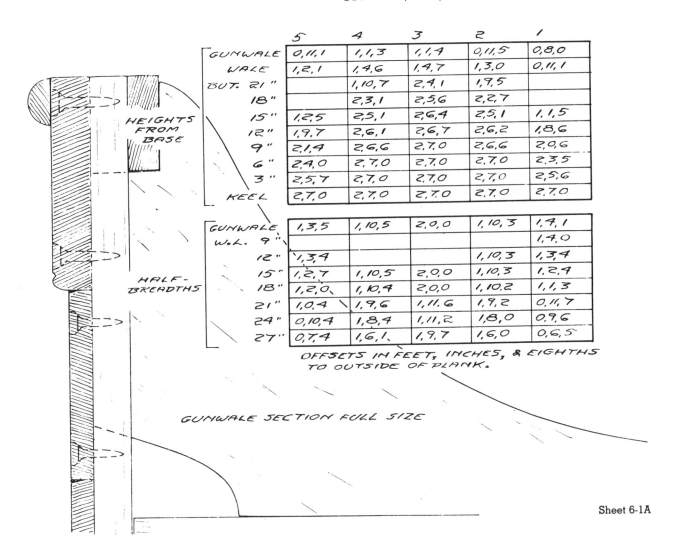

	5	4	3	2	1
GUNWALE	0,11,1	1,1,3	1,1,4	0,11,5	0,8,0
WALE	1,2,1	1,4,6	1,9,7	1,3,0	0,11,1
BUT. 21"		1,10,7	2,4,1	1,9,5	
18"		2,3,1	2,5,6	2,2,7	
15"	1,2,5	2,5,1	2,6,4	2,5,1	1,1,5
12"	1,9,7	2,6,1	2,6,7	2,6,2	1,8,6
9"	2,1,4	2,6,6	2,7,0	2,6,6	2,0,6
6"	2,4,0	2,7,0	2,7,0	2,7,0	2,3,5
3"	2,5,7	2,7,0	2,7,0	2,7,0	2,5,6
KEEL	2,7,0	2,7,0	2,7,0	2,7,0	2,7,0

HEIGHTS FROM BASE

	5	4	3	2	1
GUNWALE	1,3,5	1,10,5	2,0,0	1,10,3	1,4,1
W.L. 9"					1,4,0
12"	1,3,4			1,10,3	1,3,4
15"	1,2,7	1,10,5	2,0,0	1,10,3	1,2,4
18"	1,2,0	1,10,4	2,0,0	1,10,2	1,1,3
21"	1,0,4	1,9,6	1,11,6	1,9,2	0,11,7
24"	0,10,4	1,8,4	1,11,2	1,8,0	0,9,6
27"	0,7,4	1,6,1	1,9,7	1,6,0	0,6,5

HALF-BREADTHS

OFFSETS IN FEET, INCHES, & EIGHTHS TO OUTSIDE OF PLANK.

GUNWALE SECTION FULL SIZE

Sheet 6-1A

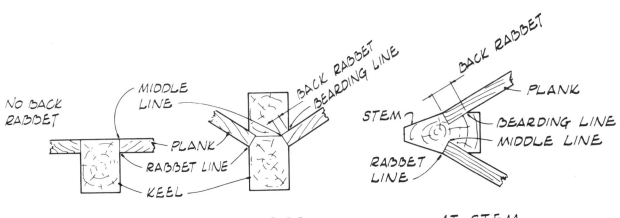

NO BACK RABBET — AMIDSHIPS

MIDDLE LINE · PLANK · RABBET LINE · KEEL · BACK RABBET · BEARDING LINE — AT GRIPE

BACK RABBET · STEM · PLANK · BEARDING LINE · MIDDLE LINE · RABBET LINE — AT STEM

BACKBONE SECTIONS

Sheet 6-1B
Not to scale.

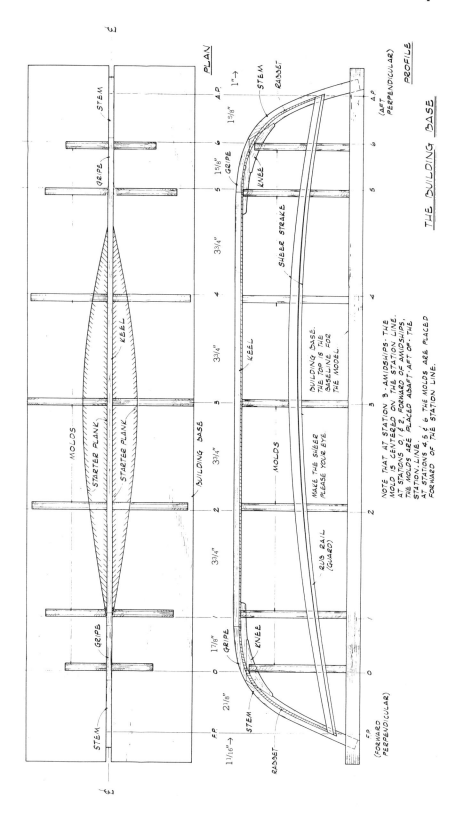

PLAN

STEM

GRIPE

GRIPE

STARTER PLANK

STARTER PLANK

KEEL

MOLDS

BUILDING BASE

GRIPE

STEM

STEM

F.P.

1 1/16" →

2 1/8"

0

1 7/8"

GRIPE

2

3 3/4"

3

3 3/4"

4

3 3/4"

5

3 3/4"

6

15/8"

A.P.

PROFILE

STEM

RABBET

1" →

KNEE

SHEER STRAKE

15/8"

KEEL

BUILDING BASE.
THE TOP IS THE
BASELINE FOR
THE MODEL.

MOLDS

MAKE THE SHEER
PLEASE YOUR EYE

RUB RAIL
(GUARD)

KNEE

STEM

RABBET

F.P.
(FORWARD
PERPENDICULAR)

A.P.
(AFT
PERPENDICULAR)

THE BUILDING BASE

NOTE THAT AT STATION 3 - AMIDSHIPS - THE
MOLD IS CENTERED ON THE STATION LINE.
AT STATIONS 0, 1 & 2, FORWARD OF AMIDSHIPS,
THE MOLDS ARE PLACED ABAFT-AFT OF THE
STATION LINE.
AT STATIONS 4, 5, & 6 THE MOLDS ARE PLACED
FORWARD OF THE STATION LINE.

Sheet 6-2
Enlarge 297 percent for full-size plans.

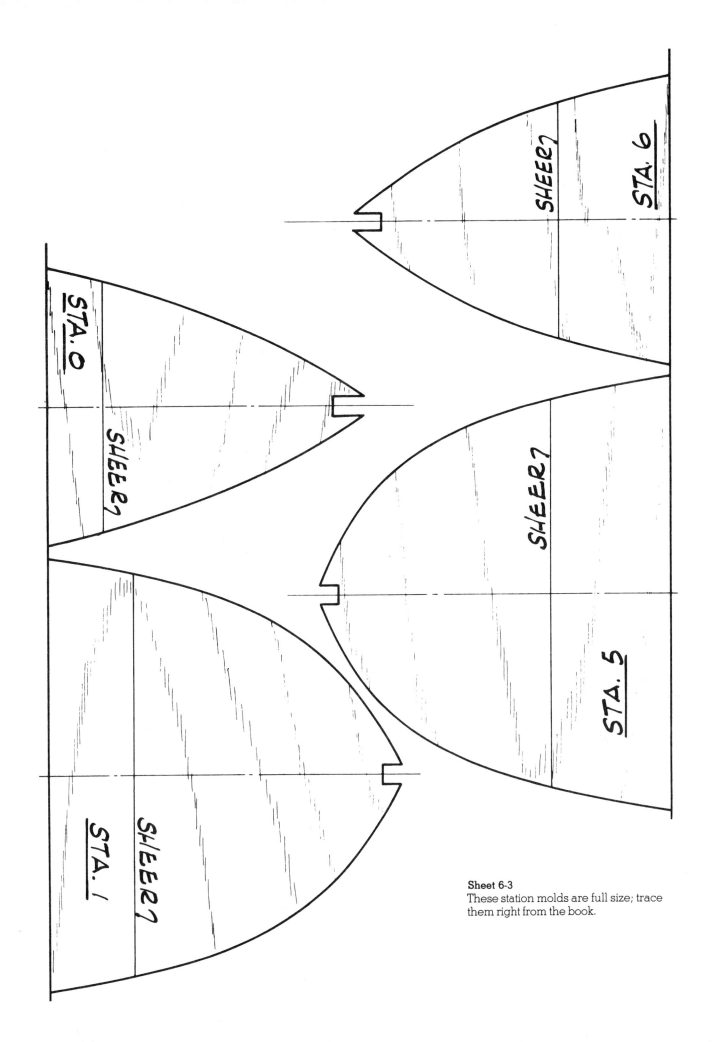

Sheet 6-3
These station molds are full size; trace them right from the book.

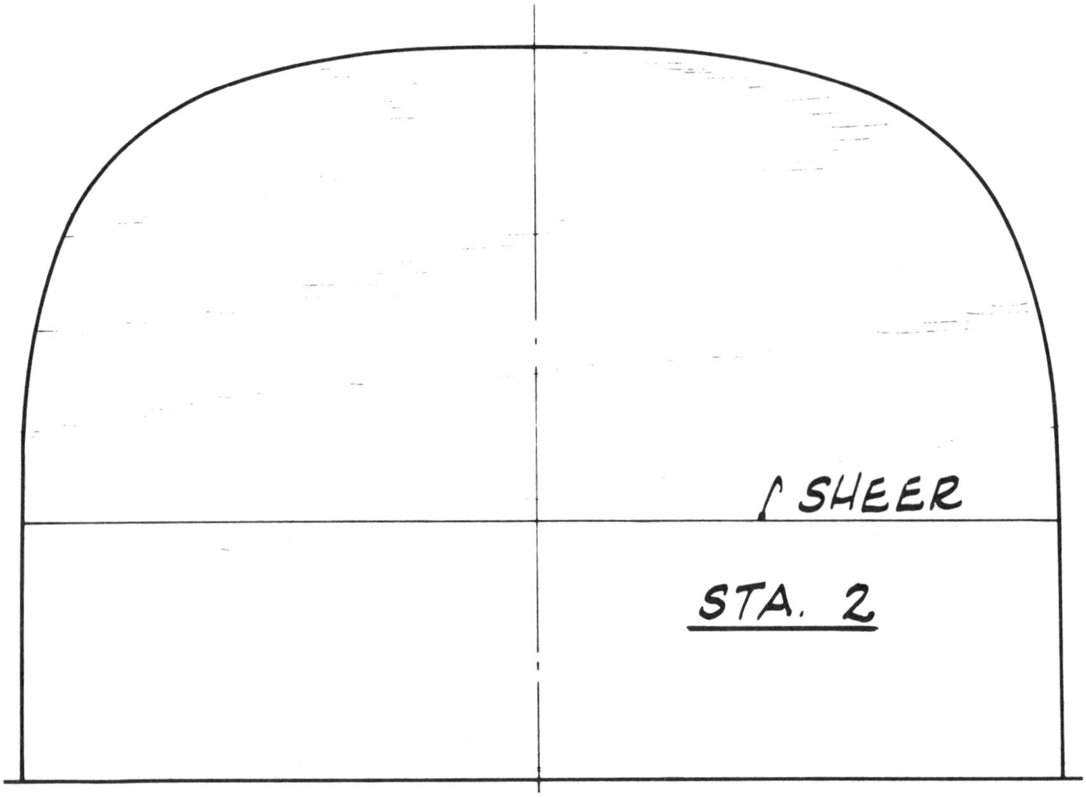

SHEER

STA. 2

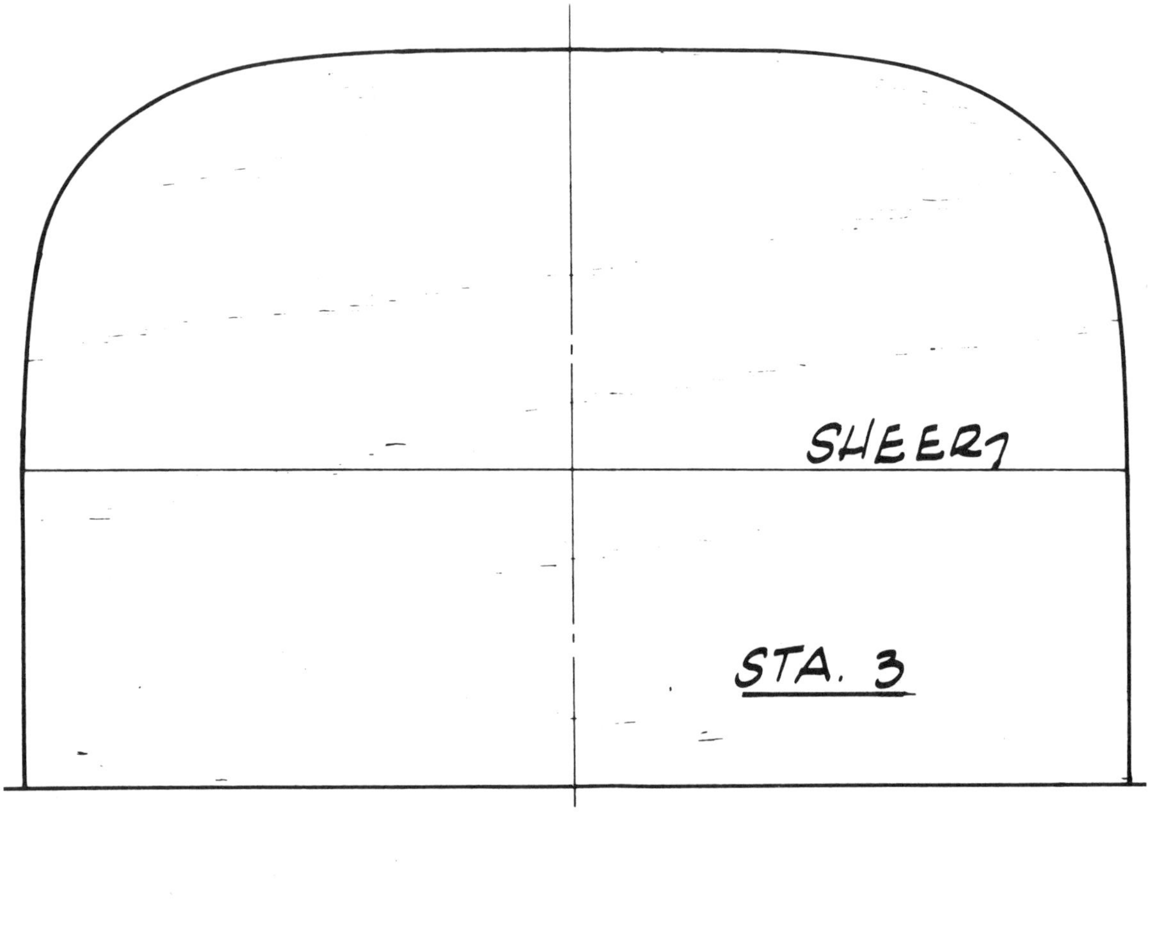

SHEER

STA. 3

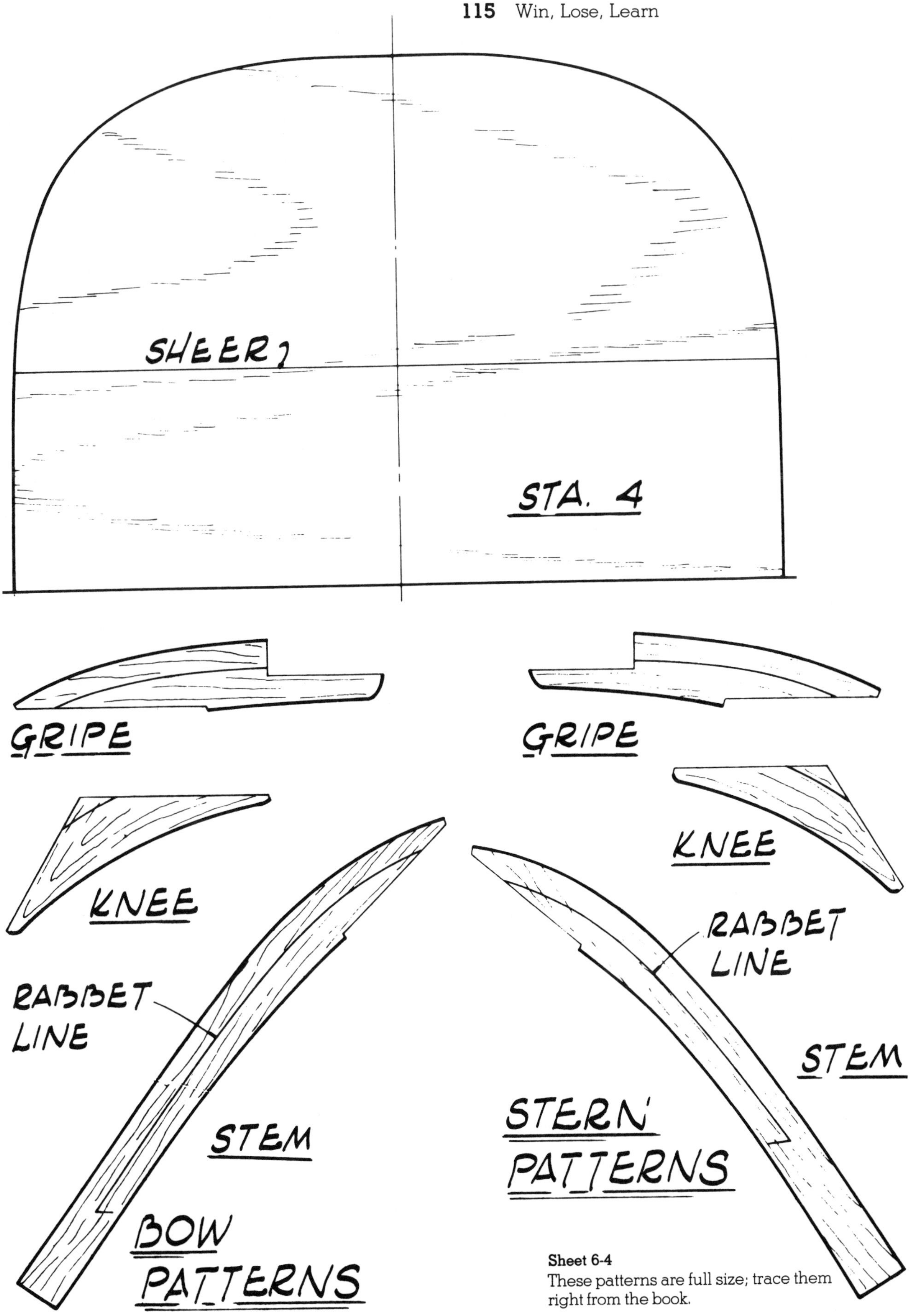

SHEER

STA. 4

GRIPE

GRIPE

KNEE

KNEE

RABBET
LINE

RABBET
LINE

STEM

STEM

BOW
PATTERNS

STERN
PATTERNS

Sheet 6-4
These patterns are full size; trace them
right from the book.

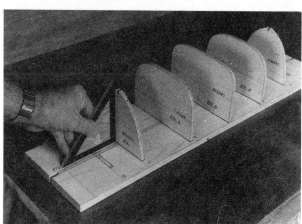

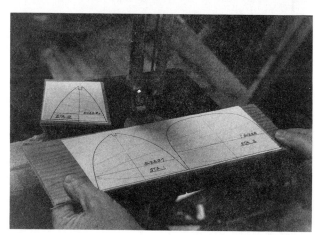

Now take a try square and square each mold station across the plywood base, *hooking the square over the edge from which you measured the centerline's location.* Take each mold and place it on the building base, being sure to note which side of the line the mold goes on. Take great pains to align the centerline on the base and the centerline marks on the mold, and carefully trace around them. Now take your rule and draw a line on each side of and parallel to the centerline, spaced exactly 3/32-inch out (measure at both ends). This represents the 3/16-inch-thick keel, and will help you align the stem and sternpost. Now you're right where you would have been if you could have found a big photocopier. Of course if you're strapped for time or just plain lazy, you can always order the full set of plans from me. See Appendix B for ordering information.

Whether you've glued the blown-up plan to the base or drawn it on, we now have a centerline in place, and the molds are all squared off and properly located. To avoid turning fore into aft, mark the A.P. (Aft Perpendicular), F.P., and all the

Clockwise from upper left: Glue the enlarged building base drawing to plywood....Glue the mold patterns to your mold stock....Saw out the molds....Position the molds on their marks, square them off, and glue them to the base.

mold station numbers on the building base. Now you need to cut a notch in each end of the base to keep the stem and sternpost accurately located during building. Take the angle directly from Sheet 6-2 with a small bevel gauge. Make the cuts that define the sides of the notch with a razor saw, being sure to leave the marks (you want a tight fit here). Unless you have an eagle eye and steady hands, hold a small square against the saw blade to ensure accuracy. End the top of the cuts precisely at the fore and aft perpendicular marks, checking the angle again with the bevel gauge, then clean out the notch with a sharp 1/8-inch chisel.

Now you're ready to glue down your mold stations. Spread some glue on their backs and plop them down on the base where indicated, checking their location with a try square—nothing to it. The building base is ready to go.

Building the Backbone

This is as good a place as any to clear up which stem is which. Properly speaking, I suppose they're both stems. Like twins, they look alike and perform the same functions, but we need to give them different names to tell them apart. We'll call the one in the stern "sternpost" and the one at the bow "stem." Let the purists howl!

In assembling the backbone, it pays to take the time to get everything properly aligned on the molds, because accuracy here is reflected straight through the whole job. Before I started this model, I was already aware of the many pitfalls for the unwary. One of them—perhaps one of the worst bugaboos facing the modelmaker—is that precision parts you have laboriously traced around have a tendency to grow. No matter how carefully you work, it's always an eye opener when you lay the parts back on the drawing—not even close.

How to get around this? Well, like Elmer, who went to the right person to help him understand boat design, I'm lucky enough to know Jay Hanna, a professional modelbuilder and marine woodcarver who lives nearby, and I went and pumped him for all I could.

How did he cut out and put together intricate assemblies, like the backbone for this peapod? I had ruined one try already and wasn't interested in ruining another. I wanted to know how to make this model's stem, sternpost, and keel assembly accurate to the plans. Jay said to cut out the paper patterns, glue them to the wood, cut out the parts, lay a piece of waxed paper over the plans, and glue them together right there on the plans. It was so simple, and it worked perfectly. Follow the same procedure for assembling this peapod's backbone, and you're nearly guaranteed an accurate job.

He also put me on the right track with such helpful hints as using quick-grabbing glue for parts that are easy to align or

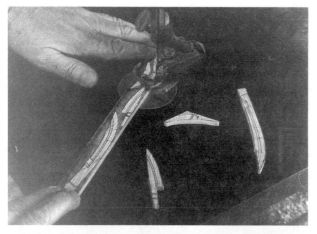

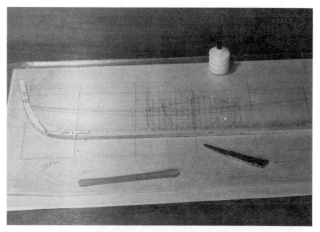

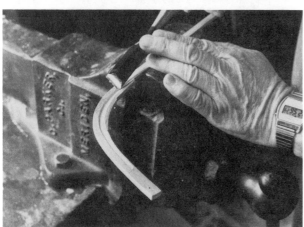

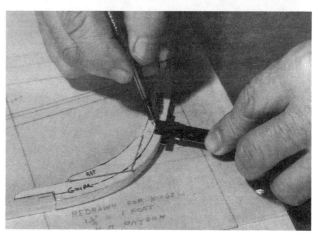

slow-grabbing glue for parts that take some fiddling; holding things together with tiny pins; and using emery boards to sand inside and outside curves.

Bolger's original plans call for a 1¹/₂-inch square keel, but when I redrew them to 1¹/₂ inch scale I enlarged the keel to 1¹/₂ inches by 2 inches (³/₁₆ x ¹/₄) to make the rabbet easier to cut, and to make the backbone a little stiffer. To make the keel, stem and sternpost, gripes, and knees, we need to find some straight, fine-grained hardwood, such as birch or maple. If you have none on hand, go to a junk store and ask around for a spare leaf from a wrecked maple drop-leaf table. That should provide enough material to make a dozen peapods.

Slice off enough ³/₁₆-inch-thick hardwood to make the backbone; you'll need about 30 running inches, the longest piece being a little more than 15 inches for the keel. Trace (or photocopy) the full-size patterns from Sheet 6-4 for the knees, the gripes, and the stem and sternpost. Move the templates around on your ³/₁₆-inch-thick wood until you find a likely looking spot that minimizes cross grain, stick down the tem-

Clockwise from upper left: Glue the backbone patterns right to wood, and saw them out....For maximum accuracy, overlay the plans with waxed paper and assemble the backbone right on top....Marking the rabbet line....Cut the rabbet with a *sharp* chisel. Match the angle of cut with the angle at which the planking meets the backbone.

plates with spray adhesive, and saw out the parts using your scroll saw or sabersaw.

Pin your full-size plans to a smooth, flat surface, overlay them with a sheet of waxed paper, and glue the parts together, making sure everything fits together properly, right on the lines. When the glue dries, mark the spot on the stem and sternpost where they bury in the base, and do any touch-up trimming with an emery board.

Try the assembled backbone on the jig (mold and base setup) to see how it fits. Set the stem and sternpost in the base up to the marks, and wedge them temporarily in place. Is the keel straight? Does it lie fair across the molds? If so, you're in business. Take off the backbone and get ready to cut the rabbet in the keel to receive the garboard, and in the stem and sternpost to receive the hood ends of the planking.

Cutting the Rabbet

The rabbet line is parallel to the faces of the stem and sternpost, which makes it fairly easy to cut. With the paper pattern in place, one side of your backbone is already marked for cutting. All you have to do is transfer that line to the unmarked side using a sharp pencil and a small marking gauge. If you don't have a marking gauge, lay a scrap of wood perpendicular to the rabbet, just touching the rabbet line, and pin and glue a scrap of wood parallel to and snugged up against the face of the stem. It should look like a lowercase "t". When it's dry, flop the backbone over, hold a sharp pencil against its end and slide it along the stem, down the keel, and up the sternpost, with the t's crossbar riding on the backbone.

Cutting the rabbet looks intimidating, but it isn't really all that bad. You have the rabbet line (where the plank enters the backbone) all marked; the bearding line (where the plank exits the backbone) needn't be that accurate. Just keep in mind that the plank always sets square to the surface it touches. If the plank comes off the mold at right angles to the keel, as it does at station 3, it butts flush against the keel. If it comes off the mold at a sharp angle, as it does at station 6, it enters the backbone at that same angle. Try a scrap piece of plank stock (1/16-inch thick for this model) an inch or so wide and several inches long against the backbone in several different places and you'll get the idea. Make the rabbet fit the plank; don't bevel the plank to fit the rabbet. You can cut the bevel by hand with a sharp, narrow chisel (about 1/8 inch) or rough it out first with a Dremel Moto-tool. Using the Dremel is risky, however, so practice on something disposable before you attack your backbone. Whichever way you decide to go, take your time and think about what you're doing.

Strip Planking

With the backbone rabbeted and all set up, you are ready to cut your plank stock. You can use cedar, pine, basswood, or whatever looks nice and is easy to work. As usual, I chose native cedar. A full-size peapod would be planked with $1\frac{1}{4}$ inch by $\frac{1}{2}$-inch-thick strips. Scaling that down for the model, to $\frac{5}{32}$ inch by $\frac{1}{16}$ inch, we'll need about 24 planks to the side, about 26 inches long. We'll also need a couple of starter planks about 1 inch wide by roughly 14 inches long; their rough shape is shown on Sheet 6-2, but we will cut them to fit later.

You can cut out all the planking on your table saw using a planer blade. Set your fence to $\frac{5}{32}$ inch and rip some straight-grained stock parallel to the grain, about 26 inches long and as deep as your saw will cut. Next set your fence to $\frac{1}{16}$ inch and run in a piece of scrap 4 or 5 inches wide and about as long as your saw table to keep these tiny planks from disappearing down the blade's slot. Lay your $\frac{5}{32}$-inch strip wide-side down and saw out as many $\frac{1}{16}$-inch-wide planks as you want. (Cut extra; you'll probably break a few.) Cutting at right angles to the grain yields a pretty, edge-grain plank. Slice it the other way and you'll end up looking at the dull, flat side. Leave the fence set to $\frac{1}{16}$ inch and saw out sufficient stock for the starter planks—an inch or so wide and 14 inches long. Lay out all the planks on a flat surface and pre-sand them with 220-grit paper mounted on a block.

In addition to the standard tool kit we've been working with right along, you'll need some specialty items, most notably "pincurl clips." Beg, borrow, or steal them from your wife or from whomever you can, but be sure to get them. They hold these planks together edgeways better than anything, can be bent to fit odd shapes, cut to size, and are unbelievably fast to use. In fact, if I hadn't had them I would never have bothered to strip plank this model. As I've mentioned, I'm a bit lazy and impatient. I didn't want to build this model badly enough to fiddle around with micro screw clamps for each one of these skinny planks. With quick-grabbing Franklin Titebond, the quicker you get the clamps on and off the quicker you can clean up glue spills, saving yourself a big job later.

And how are we going to spread glue on the edges of these tiny strips without wandering all over the place—and do it fast? With Payson's Patent Glue Spreader. Get one of those small, accordion-pleated glue bottles, cut a slot equal to your

Tools and Materials

no

yes

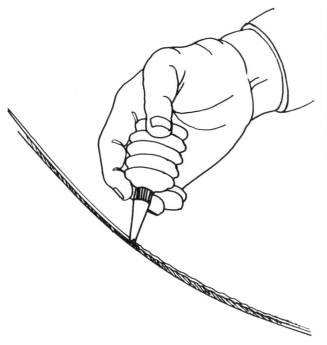

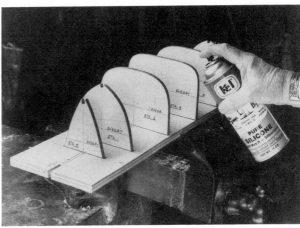

Left to right: Payson's Patent Glue Spreader in use....Wax the molds before you get started planking.

planking's thickness in the end of an electrician's wire nut, bore a hole down through the bottom of the slot to pass the glue, screw it onto your glue bottle, and you're in business—just slide it along the planks as quickly as you want.

Before we get started planking, we don't want the glued planks to stick to the molds, but we do want them to stick to the backbone. Remove the backbone from the jig and give the molds a shot of silicone spray or a few coats of wax. Now we're ready to go.

Planking

There are any number of ways to strip-plank boats. You can start at the keel, let the strips run right off the sheer any old way, then trim them flush later. Barrel-section boats with easy lines are great for this method.

With more shapely boats (like this peapod) it's necessary to spile the planking every so often—whenever it gets balky, wants to leave the molds, or requires a lot of edge setting. Fred Bates, a designer from Maine known for his strip-plank boat plans, does his spiling all at once. He starts planking at the keel, fastening the planks together temporarily, and lets the plank ends run off at random. When he gets to the turn of the bilge or thereabouts he runs a batten through the bunch, fairing them all at one crack, cuts along the line, then planks the rest of the way to the sheer with more-or-less parallel planks.

Back in 1957 I built a strip-planked Weston Farmer-designed utility outboard, the *Dolly Varden.* Mr. Farmer got his strips to run fair by using a starter, or shutter, plank. This plank had a particular shape and length which, when placed against the keel in the right place, would usually allow the builder to plank the whole boat without spiling or tapering, ending up at the sheer with a good-looking plank run. But figuring out the shape of a starter plank is no easy task.

I wanted to use a similar starter plank for this peapod, planking from it up to the sheer, but I didn't have its shape. Where there's a will there's a way, however. I did it in reverse. I started planking at the sheer, worked my way back to the keel, and found the shape of the starter plank in the process.

To get started, spring the top planks *(sheer strakes)* around the sheer marks on the molds, pinning them to each mold as you go. Spend some time on this. You might discover that strakes placed exactly on the mold's sheer marks don't please your eye. Don't hesitate to jockey them around; let your eye be the final judge. I wouldn't change the heights of the strakes at the stem and sternpost, but in between, you're the boss.

Clockwise from upper left: Hold the planks together with pincurlers while you check their fit; glue them when you're satisfied....Gang-sand a bunch of planks at once....If the 'midships planks won't lay fair, prop them out with a couple of sticks....Putting in the last strip; I've almost reached the marks for the starter planks.

Aesthetics aside, there's a practical reason for letting your eye be the final judge of the sheer line: Wood is unstable. The building base can hog or bow 1/8 inch over its length after a few days of temperature and humidity changes—particularly if the plywood was a little damp when you started. Even grain stress released by cutting the plywood to size can hurt the stability of the base.

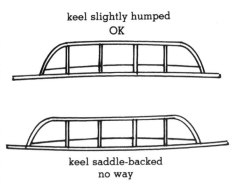

keel slightly humped
OK

keel saddle-backed
no way

Lay a steel straightedge along the keel. If you find the jig setup has changed slightly, don't panic—fix it. If the keel has bowed up a bit, adjusting the sheer line slightly should solve the problem. If it's hogged down, however, you've got bigger problems. There's an easy out, though. Slightly wet the back of the building base, clamp it to a dead-straight 2 x 4 run down the centerline, and screw it down tight with drywall screws. This will manhandle the base into shape and keep it that way. It will also give your vise something to grip if you're having trouble chasing the jig around your workbench.

To fit the sheer strake, let its ends run out by the stem and sternpost and clamp it temporarily in place. Wedge a scrap of wood between the plank and stem or sternpost and saw against that, cutting the planks to length (eyeball the rake) right on the molds. Leave them a little long, and hit the ends of the planks with an emery board until they pop right into the rabbet. Make sure the plank ends don't push against the rabbets or the planks will be forced away from the molds amidships.

Rather than glue the ends of the sheer planks into the rabbet for good, wait until you've fitted a few more planks. Three of them held together with pincurl clips will help even the run of them all. Bevel their inside edges slightly with your sanding block. When you're satisfied with their lay, glue them together for good, running your homemade glue applicator down the length of each plank and along its hood ends.

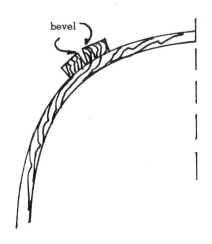

bevel

Once you get started you'll find you can hang seven strakes easily and be well on your way in far less time than you would think. Seeing the model spring alive this way will tempt you to keep going. Don't. It's "pay now or pay later"—time to start tapering the strakes.

Tapering the Planks

It will be very apparent that you are quickly closing the distance to the keel along the stem and sternpost, but there is still plenty of gap left at the 'midships mold. We need to close this gap as gracefully as possible. You will also notice that, because the stern is lower than the bow, you're closing the distance at the sternpost faster than at the stem.

We could have started tapering the ends of the strakes with the first two or three, but it wasn't really necessary. Besides, seeing the shape of a peapod emerge from thin air so quickly is too much fun to miss.

Measuring the amount of taper needed for each plank is no easy task. Fortunately, your eyeball does just as good a job—and is much easier to use. To help your eyeball along, spring a batten along the molds, halfway between your last plank and the location of the starter plank, and judge your taper from that.

Don't worry about landing exactly on the marks for the starter planks. There is no reason in the world why that plank can't be shaped a little differently. Planking from the sheer back to the keel means you are free to shut her in with whatever shape you want. Don't get hung up on precise measurements, but don't ignore them either; just try for a happy medium.

Pair a couple of strakes and set them on edge. Start tapering a little to each side of mold 3 (the widest gap to be filled). Take a few swipes with 80-grit sandpaper (remember, we want more taper aft than forward), then check on the jig. If it *looks* right, it *is* right. Do all the tapering you're going to do before fitting the ends of the planks to the rabbets, or your beautifully tapered planks will be too short. Let your eye be the judge as you try to keep the planks running parallel, first to the temporary planking batten, then to the marks for the starter planks.

When you get to the turn of the bilge, or perhaps a little before, you will notice that the planks are increasingly reluctant to lie in fair against the molds. So far, the planks have needed very little twist in their run. It's another story now. The hood ends of the planks are nearly plumb on the stem and sternpost, but almost flat amidships.

This is where the fun begins. Aside from being tapered, each plank is twisted nearly 90 degrees twice along its length. To put this much shape in the planks you'll need to soak them. You could throw them into a homemade tank, or wrap them in damp paper towels, but there's an easier way. There was a picture in *WoodenBoat* magazine a while ago of a kayak-building Eskimo chomping a piece of wood. This was a boatbuilder who knew where to find a constant supply of warm water. Take a cue from experience, and soak a mouthful of planks while you taper a pair. Soak them, twist them, taper them, bevel and pin them—anything to get them in place. If the planks want to flatten out between molds, push them to a fair curve with a couple of braced sticks.

When you reach the marks for the starter planks, remove the temporary fastenings that secure the stem and sternpost, and pry each mold away from the base with a chisel. Turn the model rightside up. Hold the starter plank stock (I suppose shutter plank is a more accurate description, but let's not fly in

Planking Finale

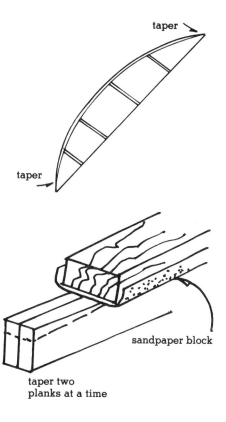

taper

taper

sandpaper block

taper two planks at a time

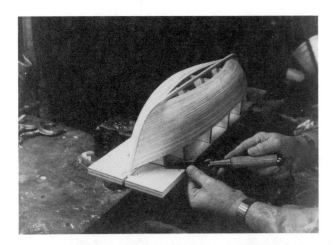

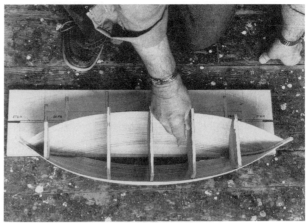

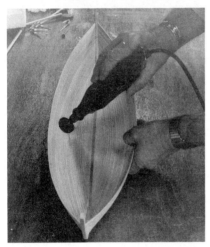

the face of tradition) under the hull, right against the keel, and trace each plank's shape from inside the hull—so easy you almost feel guilty about it. Cut them out, glue them in, and she's planked.

Congratulate yourself and gloat a moment; the model is half done. With her stiff bottom and hard bilges, this peapod is not the easiest shape in the world to plank. You might not do it to suit the first time, but so what? Speaking from my own experience, I don't think I've ever made a boat model without seeing that I could do the next one a little better. If we knew we were going to do everything right the first time, wouldn't that take away the fun of experimenting and learning?

Before you go on to the next step, sanding the outside of the hull, take a hard look at the planking. Do you see any planks that are slightly out of line? If so, carefully insert a razor blade in the joint and pry it gently apart (the glue will give way). Reglue the planks, holding them in line with your fingers until the glue grabs. If you try to sand down those uglies, you may sand right through the hull.

Clockwise from upper left: When the glue dries on the last plank, pry the molds away from the building base....Trace the shape of the starter planks on your plank stock....Sand the hull smooth by hand....Sand the inside of the hull with a small power sander.

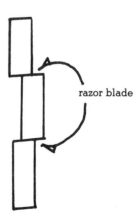

razor blade

Glue the molds back to the base and set the hull back on it. If you trust yourself, mow the planks down fair with a disc sander. If you have never used one before, this probably isn't the place to learn. Instead, use a variable-speed drill with sandpaper no coarser than 80-grit. A variable-speed drill can turn slowly enough to let you see what you are doing before you've done it—like putting deep scratches in the hull—something likely to happen with a fast, constant-speed drill. The safest way, of course, is to sand the old-fashioned way: by hand.

Sanding the inside of the hull is tougher. This is where power sanding with a small disc sander shines. I bought a special shaft attachment for my Dremel Moto-tool for a few bucks, and spent another few for a bunch of 3/4-inch diameter, medium-coarse sanding discs. These were too small, too fine, and proved useless for the job. The shaft was right, however, so I made my own 1 3/8-inch diameter discs from 50-grit sandpaper, which worked well. Even at its half-speed of 15,000 r.p.m., sanding with this tool was tricky. Don't linger in one spot; keep it moving and use a light touch, or buy a variable-speed Dremel. Finish sanding—inside and out—with 220-grit paper, followed by 320.

Adding the Gunwales

Before we get to framing and finishing the hull's interior, we need to stiffen her with a pair of gunwales. Ordinarily, you frame out a full-size boat before you put on the gunwales, but this boat's planking is a bit delicate, and you could use the gunwales' help during framing.

I wanted to show off the boat's sheer with darker gunwales, so I made mine from a couple of 3/4-inch by 1 1/4-inch (3/32 x 5/32) strips of mahogany. If you're short of mahogany, use what you have on hand—birch, maple, whatever—and stain it to suit. A little cordovan shoe polish works well.

Most hardwoods, particularly mahogany, are quite stiff, so either soak them Eskimo style, or wrap them in ammonia-soaked paper towels for an hour or so. Bend them right around the molds to let them get used to the idea, and let them sit until they dry.

While you're waiting for the gunwales to develop a memory, seal the inside of the hull with a coat of thinned varnish. Why now? We're about to start gluing the frames into the hull. Glue tends to stain the planking, leaving ugly white spots to mar your varnish job. The glue from the frames won't penetrate the varnish, so spilled glue can be wiped up immediately with a damp rag. One coat of sealer varnish doesn't spoil the glue bond. If my models fall apart a hundred years from now, I won't worry about it. Chances are, no museum will be embarrassed either.

When the gunwales dry, glue them in place along the sheer, carefully keeping the gunwales' top edges flush with the top of the planking. Glue is slippery, and these gunwales are subjected to a lot of bending and twisting. You'll need quite a few clamps to hold them in place.

(Speaking of clamps, just by chance I received in the mail a sample of what have become the best clamps I've ever used. They are hand made by the R. Ullom Co., of Orwell, Vermont—specialists in clamps for violin makers and other special trades. The clamps are made of aluminum, have knurled adjustment screws with adjustable brass pads, and are first class in every way.)

Fill any uglies on the outside of the hull with Duratite plastic wood dough. If your cans are like mine, when you open one looking for a well-moistened tad to fill a tiny blemish, you'll find the dough hardened and quite useless. You can bring this unyielding, dismal-looking lump back to life by adding a little acetone. I've yet to have a can so dry I couldn't resurrect it.

With your uglies filled, sand the hull and flow on a sealing coat of varnish to protect it from fingerprints, glue drips, etc. Make a notched stick to span the hull at the gunwales amidships to hold her shape when we put in the frames.

Fitting Out the Interior

Framing

Finishing the hull's interior calls for bent frames, or timbers, if you like. A strip-built boat doesn't need that many; the planking is plenty strong by itself. But timbers look sharp in a model, so in they go.

Make them from birch, maple—most any fine-grained hardwood—1 inch by 3/4 inch (1/8 x 3/32), 11 inches long. You'll need 23, but make a few extra to compensate for breakage. Lay them in a bunch on a flat surface and mark a centerline down the lot so you'll be able to center them on the keel.

You're asking a lot of these skinny strips of hardwood, torturing them into this peapod's hard bilges. Unless you have good, supple, bending wood, soaking them Eskimo style probably won't work. Instead, split a piece of 1¼-inch (or thereabouts) plastic pipe lengthwise, plug the ends with wood, fill it with household ammonia, and soak the timbers for a few hours or overnight. I did this, and made the timbers so supple I could, and did, tie a knot in one of them.

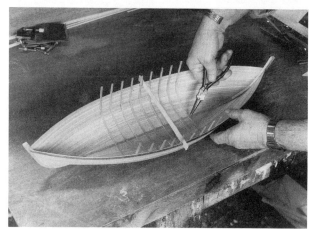

Clockwise from upper left: Stretch your soaked timbers first...then let them dry in mold cavities. Note the homemade timber soaker: split PVC pipe plugged with wood....Mark the frames' location in the boat. Note the spreader to keep her gunwales spaced correctly.

Rather than put in the timbers soaking wet, which wouldn't do much for the glue bond, I prebent my frames in three mold cavities made from scrap ends of 2 x 6, each representing a different section of the boat. Since I used the stiffest aft sections—molds 3, 4, and 5—frames bent in these also fit the forward sections of the boat. Take a frame from the tank and bend it around something round, such as an aerosol can, to stretch the wood fibers evenly. Push its center down in the middle of number 3 cavity, pin or hold the frame in place, and overbend the frame's top so that when it springs back against the cavity's side, the fiber's tension is released. Why? Because a bunch of frames with a lot of outward tension at their tops are of no help in retaining the boat's shape. It works the other way, too. You can bend them too much, and when they dry and harden, they won't want to pull in to the boat's side. Bend a few and you'll see.

To make framing easier, we will put in the frames, mark their locations along the keel and sheer, take them out, saw them in two, and put them back in. What's so easy about that?

Well, by cutting them in half so they butt on the keel, you need wrestle only half a frame into place instead of a whole one. There's a structural advantage, too. I learned about this the hard way.

Alton Whitmore, an old-time North Haven Island boatbuilder long since gone to his reward, built a small wherry—with these two-piece frames—that I lobstered out of back in the early Fifties. I was thinking about going into the boatbuilding business at the time, so I spent a lot of time thinking about boats, and wondered why Alton didn't just bend in one-piece frames. It seemed much easier.

I found out why later. I built a strip-planked boat from bone-dry pine, ignoring the old man's way of framing, and bent in her frames one piece, rail to rail. I took it to a boat show in Rockland, but it didn't sell, so I hauled the boat home, threw a tarp over it, and kept it on a trailer in the yard. I lifted the tarp after a rainstorm and, although there was very little water in the boat, every frame had pulled free of the planks, leaving unbelievable gaps. I could stick a finger between the frames and the planks at the hard turn of the bilge. I had to retimber the whole boat because I hadn't realized that wood boats grow, and something, somewhere, has to give.

Alton Whitmore knew it, and did something about it. He butted his frames on the keel so that when the planks swelled the frames could stretch apart. The floor timbers spaced halfway between each pair of frames made up for any strength lost by the two-part frames.

I should have realized that the old boatbuilders knew what they were doing and followed their lead. I didn't, however, and it cost me. I demonstrated this same boat to a prospective buyer later, and it was sinking the whole time—hardly a good way to start a boatbuilding career!

For another bit of wisdom from the old-time builders, forget about putting in the frames all nice and square to the keel and sides, as they're shown in Sheet 6-1. That's easy enough for the architect to do on his drawing board, but just try doing it on the boat. Let the frames' tops swing naturally to the face of the planking and save yourself the trouble of twisting and torturing them into place. You may need to twist them a little to get them to lie flat to the planks, but if you avoid timber twisting as much as possible you'll have an easier, stronger, betterlooking job. The old timers did it that way, so (finally) it's good enough for me.

We'll start framing amidships, working in both directions toward the ends of the hull—the same way you would do it in a full-size boat. Measuring along the keel from dead amidships (station 3), mark the frame's location every 7 ($7/8$) inches. Mea-

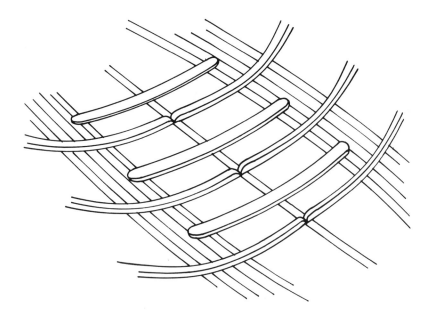

The floor timbers stiffen the bottom, and make up for the strength lost by the two-part frames.

sure along the top of the sheer strake towards the bow from station 3 to see how the frames will look as you approach the bow. Make a paper pattern with the approximate frame locations ticked off. This is better than trusting your eye; if the frame spacing doesn't suit you, you can easily adjust them all for position and looks before gluing them in. This worked well for me, and saved me from last-minute fiddling.

When you figure out the spacing, glue all the frames in place, working both ways from the center. Fill any gaps between the frames and the planks with glue, wiping up any excess immediately with a damp rag. If you can't reach a spot with a rag, use the point of a knife or a small, *sharp* chisel.

Cut out the floor timbers next. These should be 2 (1/4) inches wide, 1 (1/8) inch thick, and long enough to span the flat area of the boat's bottom. Their length isn't crucial, but they should not run up into the turn of the bilge. On a real boat, the ends of the floors will tend to straighten out as the boat flexes, and will try to push the planks off the boat.

The floor timbers will look best if you adjust their length to follow the curve of one of the planks fairly near the keel, keeping the timbers reasonably short near the ends of the boat where great strength is not needed. Cut them a little long, try them between the frames to find the best position, and mark their locations and their ends for trimming.

Take out the floors, round their ends with sandpaper, spread some glue on their backs, put them back in, and we're through framing. We will let the frame tops stand uncut until the breasthooks and the inside gunwales (clamps) are in, then we will cut them off and fair everything in together.

Give the frames a coat of varnish so the glue from the seat risers won't stain them. I forgot to do this, and have slight stains to remind me until next time.

You can scale the locations and heights for the seat risers right off the plans (Sheet 6-1), although their locations are not crucial. They don't follow the sheer, but run straight, higher at the bow than at the stern, from station 1 to station 5. Measure down from the gunwales, 8 (1) inches amidships, $10^1/2$ ($1^5/16$) inches at station 1, and 11 ($1^3/8$) inches at station 5, and mark these locations on the frames.

Seats and Risers

Cut the risers from *straight-grain* hardwood, $5/8$ inch by $1^1/2$ ($5/32$ x $3/16$) inches, to the approximate length (leave them a little long), and bend them temporarily in place along the marks. Take a look and see how they set. They tend to look out of whack because they don't follow the planks' run, so you will have to rely on your eyes. Some builders found all this to be too much of a job, and just let the risers run with the sheer. The seats and risers don't look half bad that way. But if the boat had much sheer, objects placed on the seats tend to slide off—bad news if it's your morning cup of coffee or a tub of greasy bait.

Bevel the tops of the risers to follow the flare of the sides. This provides a flat surface to support the seats and helps the risers bend in more easily. You may need to soak them as well, as these strips won't be too happy about taking an inside bend.

Make sure every frame is marked with the location of the risers, spot each frame with a dab of glue, stick the risers in, and hold them in place with your fingers or sticks braced off to the opposite side of the boat until the glue grabs.

The seats are 11 ($1^3/8$) inches wide by $3/4$ ($3/32$) inch thick. Take their locations from the plan and mark where they go on the tops of the seat risers. Make a stand-in extension rule from two sticks and a clamp, and measure the distance from frame to frame at the fore-and-aft end of each seat. As is always the case when fitting things around a boat, *cut the seats longer*, then scribe fit them with dividers to butt against the frames. Give the seats a sealing coat of varnish to protect them from glue stains.

Breasthooks

If you forget about using a rule and trust your eyes, breasthooks are quite easy to make. I remember feeding my first attempts to my shop stove over thirty years ago. I must have learned something since then, however, because both of these fit the 'pod on the first try. Follow along and yours should fit right the first time too.

What's right? Take a look at the plan view on Sheet 6-1 and the photographs here. Note how the breasthooks flow nicely

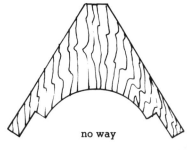

A breasthook made from straight-grain wood will have little strength compared with a two-piece breasthook.

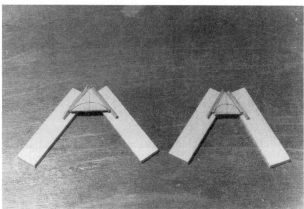

Left to right: The breasthook template in place. Note the four pieces of frame scrap. These ensure an easy fit around the timbers and stem....Trying out the templates on the breasthook stock.

along the planking, how they're notched around the stems, and how the inside gunwales blend into the notch in the breasthook's aft end. Note also how the breasthooks are mitered on the centerline, how they're curved to flow into the gunwales in a way most pleasing to the eye. For a breasthook, that's *right.*

To get started, cut four scrap pieces of frame stock (two to each side) to fit between the last set of frames and the stem, shaving the bow ends so they fit snugly. These two frame scraps represent the combined thickness of the frames and gunwales. Clamp them in place temporarily; you've just established the breasthook's shape and taken the first step toward making an accurate template.

Cut the inboard frame scrap a few inches short (about 1/4 inch) to provide a landing spot for the inside gunwale, and glue the frame scraps together (but not to the boat!). Lock this assembly together, right in the boat, with a scrap triangle of wood fitted between the frame scraps. Cut it roughly to shape and finish fitting it with a file and sandpaper. You'll have to bevel its edges to get it snug against the scraps, which follow the boat's flare. When it fits snugly between the scraps, glue it to them and you've got a template.

Remove the template from the boat when the glue dries, and we're ready to swing the arc. Don't worry about getting this right the first time. We're just using a pencil, and an eraser can easily get you out of trouble. Estimate the breasthook's depth from the aft face of the stem along the centerline—nothing fussy here, but we do need enough depth to swing a pleasing arc. My model's breasthooks are 5½ (¹¹/₁₆) inches deep at the bow and 6 (³/₄) inches deep at the stern, measured from the breasthook's throat to the stem or sternpost.

Draw a straight line 4 or 5 inches long and center your template on it by eye. Stick the leg of the dividers on the centerline and swing an arc that flows from gunwale to gunwale, or, in this case, from one short scrap of framing to the other. Adjust the gap of the dividers until it looks *right*. When it does, repeat the whole process for the other breasthook. You'll find this one a lot easier.

If you've gotten this far you've got it made—or at least you're close. At this point you might ask, "Why go to the trouble of making a two-piece breasthook when I could do it in one shot, one piece?" The answer is simple: *grain*.

No boatbuilder worth his shavings would ever make a breasthook in one piece from straight-grain wood; it would have absolutely no strength. The short slash grain across those small ends would likely break before he got it in the boat. A mitered breasthook isn't as strong as a one-piece breasthook made from a natural crook, but I always figured it was a lot easier to put up with that than to run around the forest looking for the perfect root, digging it up, chopping it out, cutting it to shape, then waiting a year or so for it to dry.

Now that we have the two breasthook templates, let's look at materials. Because it's fine-grained, easy to work, and readily available, I chose birch, both for the breasthooks and the inside gunwales. The gunwales are ³/₄ inch (³/₃₂) by 1¼ (⁵/₃₂) inches, and the breasthooks need to be a dite thicker—perhaps ¹/₆₄ inch—to allow for the crown. Look at station 1 on Sheet 6-1 and you'll notice that the breasthook curves up from both gunwales. It isn't much, but that crown adds a lot to the looks compared with a breasthook dead-flat across.

Cut two pieces of the stock you've chosen 7 (⁷/₈) inches wide by a strong 1¼ (³/₁₆) inches thick, and long enough to make both breasthooks. Angle them together to match the shape of the breasthook template, lay a straight-edge scrap the same width over the pieces, and mark where it crosses them. Cut along the marked lines, then glue the two pieces together.

Lay the templates on the stock upside down (this takes into consideration the angle of the side flare, which was built in when you first made the template) and mark their shapes carefully. Keep trying the breasthooks for fit after an initial rough test, using a delicate sand-and-try approach. The extra thickness of the breasthook should protrude above the sheer for

Clockwise from upper left: Marking the miter on the breasthook stock....Swing an arc that flows from gunwale to gunwale. Note the sides angled to follow the boat's flare....Clamp the inside gunwales tight against the timbers before cutting them to length.

now. We'll cut the crown later. Shape the notch where the breasthook butts against the stem with a needle file.

Place the mitered joint on the line you drew earlier and swing the dividers—just as you did for the templates—for the breasthooks' curves. Cut them out with a scroll saw or a jeweler's saw, then cut the notches to receive the inside gunwales. You can angle these cuts, which will make the inside gunwales a little easier to fit, or you can cut them square across as I did. This makes it a little harder to fit the inside gunwales, but I think it's better looking. A little tinkering for final fit and that does it; glue them in.

Fitting the inside gunwales to the breasthooks looks simple: just cut them to length between two points. Unfortunately, it isn't quite that easy. If they aren't held in tight against the timbers for their entire run, they'll come up short, matched to the notch in the breasthook, when you make the end cut. Best to cut them a little long and sandpaper-fit their ends until they snap right in. Don't glue them yet, but mark them so you'll know which is port and which is starboard—they're not interchangeable.

Finishing the Hull

gunwale flows into breasthook

Before we go any further, we need to make a crowning board to draw the deck crown. I first saw one of these simple and elegant tools in Sam Rabl's classic, *Boatbuilding in Your Own Backyard* (Cornell Maritime Press, 1958). Draw a straight line 5 feet (7½ inches) long and erect a 2-inch-high (¼) perpendicular line midway across. Stick in pins at the 2-inch mark and at each end. Place a couple of sticks against the end pins, letting them cross at the center pin, and glue them together. Remove the center pin, substitute a pencil, and with the legs of the sticks bearing on the end pins, move the whole shebang along with the pencil held at the apex, thus drawing your crown. (The sticks must be long enough to make the arc without running off the pins.) Cut it out and you're ready to go.

Lay your crowning board across the sheer and bring the inside gunwales up to it along the length of the boat, marking the locations on the frames as you go. Keep checking the end-fit of your gunwales. They love to slip silently out of place as you put them in, hoping not to be noticed until they're glued down nice and tight.

Clockwise from upper left: Making a crowning board. Stick your pencil right where the sticks cross and slide it along on the pins: instant deck crown....
Cut out the crowning board and bring up the inside gunwales flush with it. Mark the timberheads for cutting (leave them a little long)....Mow down the timberheads with sandpaper mounted on a rounded block of wood....Brace the center thwart with a knee notched around the inside gunwale.

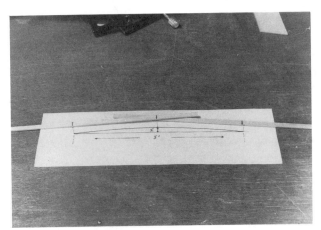

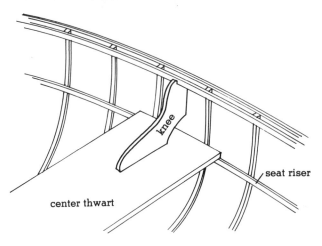

After the gunwales are in, all that's left is to cut the frames flush with the gunwales, sand their ends, and fair everything together in a pleasing flow of lines. The safest way to cut off the frames is with a razor saw. That was too slow for me, so I did it on my table saw with a planer blade set just high enough to make the cut. If you aren't at least 99 percent confident in your abilities, don't try it; one mis-flicker and you've lost the whole show.

To avoid marring the gunwales or planking with the saw, leave the frames about 1/16 inch high and bring them down flush with a curved sanding block and 80-grit sandpaper. Why curved? A straight-bottom block would hang up against the frames you've yet to mow down. Crown the breasthooks with the sanding block (check their curve with the crowning board) and finish sanding with 220-, then 320-grit sandpaper.

Make a pair of knees, which can be scaled directly from the plans (Sheet 6-1), to support the center seat, or thwart. These fit against the planking, and are notched around the inner gunwale. Make them from scraps of leftover breasthook stock; if the grain is curved, so much the better.

The last job is to taper the stem and sternpost. Draw centerlines on the face of both, running them down almost to the keel. Draw two parallel lines on each, 3/8 (3/64) inch from the centerline, so that you end up with 3/4-inch (3/32) stem faces. Taper to these lines with sandpaper on a block (be careful not to hit the hull planking) and with a small, sharp chisel. Use the chisel as a scraper, being careful not to wobble as you go. We want the line from the rabbet to the face of the stem or sternpost to remain straight. As you near the forefoot (the lower part of the stem and sternpost), gradually widen the taper until it fairs gracefully into the keel.

Cut off the stemheads to suit your taste; some leave them long, cocked a little higher forward than the sheer; some cut them flush with the sheer. Whichever way you go this is the final finishing touch; you've made one pretty model.

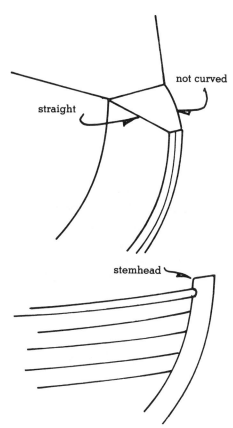

Oars and Oarlocks? Why Not?

Well, almost the final touch. Oars and oarlocks really do it. The exquisite job Elmer did with his—right down to the tiny keeper holes in his oarlocks—really inspired me. And two pairs of oars! Having made neither oars nor oarlocks, I was reluctant to start now. But after seeing how well my model came out, it seemed worth the try. I'm glad I did! When people look at the model and ask, "Where did you get the oarlocks?" I can say, "I made them!"

Like everything else in the boat, oars and oarlocks must be in scale or they stick out like a sore toe. To ensure accuracy, I scaled both down from the full-size article. Making these tiny

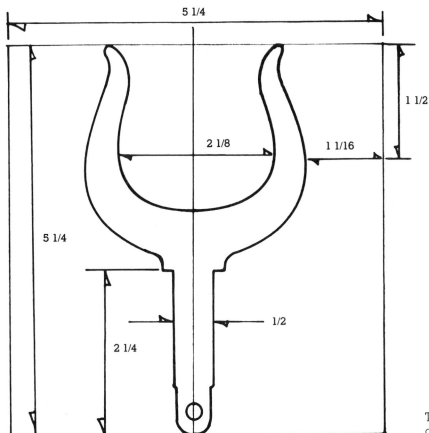

actual size

The peapod's oarlock; measured drawing and actual size for the model.

oarlocks took some thought. Of what will I make them? How shall I shape them? With what tools? How will I hold these tiny suckers while I work on them?

I scaled the oarlocks from a **#**1 Wilcox Crittenden Boston-type oarlock by measuring its overall dimensions in real inches and translating that down to 1½ inches to the foot with my scale rule. You could do the same thing by laying the oarlock on graph paper and tracing around it.

I made a wooden pattern from the reduced drawing, laid it on the sheet brass—part of an old brass door stool found at a lawn sale, worn thin (to about 3/32 inch) by years of feet tramping over it—and traced around it with a sharp awl. I drilled the large holes for the oar while the parts were still in place and easy to hold. There was no way I could cut a full circle that small, so I made a series of cuts close to the line using a fine-toothed, ½-inch bandsaw blade, each cut removing brass equal to the thickness of the blade.

Next, I drilled holes for the keepers. I used the finest drill, a **#**80 (0.0135 inch), chucked in a Dremel Moto-tool. There's a

More Metalsmithery

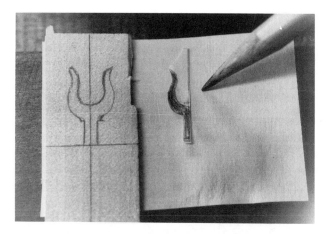

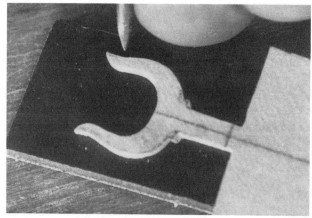

method to this madness. Drill the holes first and you can work the oarlock shanks down to match them. No way would I try to center and drill the hole after the tiny shanks were turned round.

Finish the oarlocks with a chainsaw file, needle files—whatever it takes—and sandpaper of the finest grit you can find. A buffing wheel, or just a rag and some rubbing compound, will give you a nice polish.

Making these little critters took a couple of days. But with the model sitting there begging for them, what's two days? If I were to make a lot of this small hardware, however, I'd buy a modelbuilder-size bandsaw. Micro-Mark shows one in their catalog that is supposed to cut wood up to 3½ inches thick, and metal—aluminum or brass—up to ¼-inch thick. My 10-inch Delta bandsaw will do this as well, but there is no way I can use those 1/16-inch bandsaw blades, so I have to be innovative around those tight curves with a series of redundant straight cuts.

Those tool catalogs can be addicting. I see so much in them to make a modeler's life easy that I'm tempted to load

Clockwise from upper left: Make a wooden pattern for the oarlock. To ensure symmetry, trace half, flop it over, and trace the other half....Scribe the oarlock's shape on sheet brass with a sharp awl....Cut the oarlocks roughly to shape; finish with files and sandpaper....Rabbet the brass oarlock plates into the wooden oarlock mounts.

myself down with a shopful of equipment. Perhaps later in life I will, as my fascination with modelbuilding grows.

Scale the locations for the oarlock mounts from the plans. Make the mounts from scraps of wood 3/4 (3/32) inch by 2 (1/4) inches by 8 or 9 (1 1/8 or 1 1/4) inches (you'll need four). Make four small brass oarlock plates, and rabbet the mounts so they will sit flush. I didn't have a chisel small enough for this job so I ground an old screwdriver to the correct size and shape. Drill the holes to receive the oarlock shanks with a 1/64-inch drill, and fit them to the shanks with a tapered reamer. Glue the brass plates to the mounts and this job is done.

Oars

I scaled the 8-foot oars from a favorite pair I bought from Shaw & Tenney, of Orono, Maine—makers of very nice oars. Scale the oars just the way you did the oarlocks: Measure the overall length in real feet, draw a centerline with your scale rule, and establish as many reference points as you need to help define the oar's shape. Draw a plan view looking straight on, draw a profile view, and cut out the resulting paper pattern.

I took about a day and a half to make my oars, with some time allotted to the scaling process, some to laying them out, and quite a bit to just sitting and thinking about how I was going to make them. I made each oar from fine-grained birch stock, 1 1/2 (3/16) inches by 6 (3/4) inches, 8 (1) feet long.

Lay your paper pattern on the stock, trace around it, and saw out the oar square-edge on the bandsaw. I thought rounding the loom would be the hard part so I did that first, before finishing the blade, to see if I could do it right (not egg

Oarmaking, full size. Courtesy Shaw & Tenney, Orono, Maine.

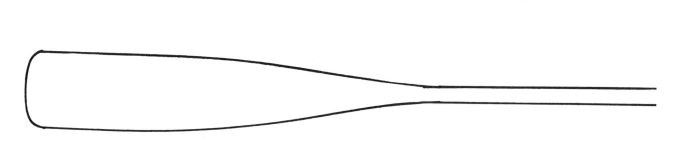

shaped!). I didn't want to chance throwing out a beautifully crafted blade because I ruined the loom. Round the loom between the blade and the grip by filing it 8-sided, then 16-sided, then rounding it with sandpaper.

Rounding the loom was no trouble at all; neither was tapering the blade. I took a cue from the dedicated worker in Shaw & Tenney's ad—the gent you see intently grinding down a blade on that big drum sander—and did it the same way on my 8-inch coarse grinding wheel, which struck my eye as bearing the same scale relationship to Shaw & Tenney's sanding drum as did my miniature oar and their full-size one. That fellow would be pleased; it worked perfectly. I finished the job with sandpaper and varnish. The oars look great, they fit the oarlocks, they both fit the boat, and I continue to gloat over the whole project. I didn't know I could do it until I tried.

Full-size pattern for oars. Trace these directly from the book.

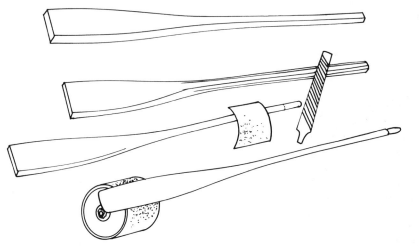

Oarmaking, model size.

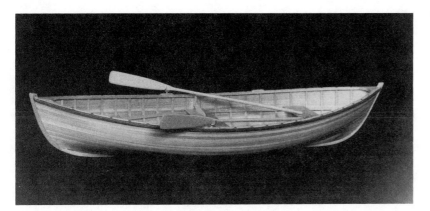

The finished peapod, ready for a row.

For Those Who Must

Since the primary reason for planking is to keep water out, it doesn't matter whether it's carvel, lapstrake, or strip—strip being easiest. For a hard-bilged hull like this peapod, about the only reason to carvel plank is to prove to yourself that you can do it. Of course well-lined-off carvel planking is a delight to the eye. I suppose that could be enough to push the undecided over the edge.

Carvel planking at any scale is fussy work. My initial failure with Elmer's method can be attributed—at least in part—

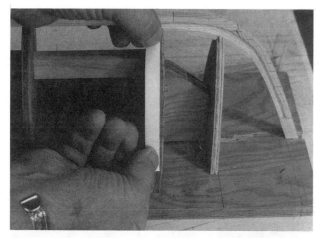

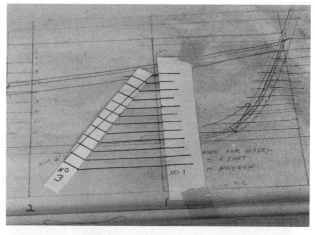

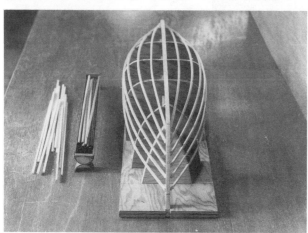

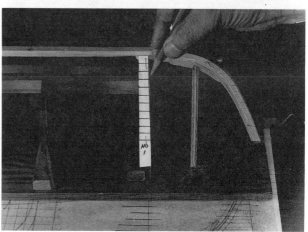

to not taking the time to accurately locate the heights of the planks on the stem and sternpost, or to accurately determine the widths of the planks at each mold station. Going from full-size boats to miniature ones is quite a switch. It never occurred to me that all those things have to be that accurate in a model.

I made another attempt at carvel planking this peapod, but lost interest when the idea for strip planking came to me. As the to-be-carvel-planked model now stands, she's ribbanded, timbered, the planking is lined off, and she's all ready to plank when time and patience allows. Perhaps some day I'll get back to it, if I can stop building other models long enough. If you have a burning desire to learn the carvel-planking process, this peapod is a good place to start. It'll never get much harder. Figure on twice the time compared to strip planking, and twice the work.

We start with the building base, molds, and rabbeted backbone set up just as for strip planking. In a nutshell, the subsequent steps in any carvel-planking job are to determine the

Clockwise from upper left: Run a paper strip between the lower edge of the wale and the rabbet. (This is station 1; the key strip—station 3—was done earlier, offstage.)...Swing the key strip until its top and bottom marks fit between the top and bottom marks of the station you're figuring. Mark the plank-width lines straight across....Transfer the plank-width markings to the molds; run pairs of ribbands along the molds for every other plank....The hull with all its ribbands, waiting for the timbers to soak.

Carvel Planking 101

plank widths at each mold, working down from the sheer. (The more precisely you do this, the easier your planking job will be.) Fasten a thin strip, or *ribband*, along the line of each plank, adjusting them until they run fair. Bend frames, or *timbers*, inside the ribbands, fastening them temporarily. Then replace the ribbands with shaped planks, one pair at a time.

The first job is to put on the sheer ribband, sawn from straight-grain, 1-inch-square (⅛) stock. Shift the ribband around to suit your eye all you like, though I'd keep the heights the same at the stem and sternpost. When you're satisfied, mark the sheer line. Now run another batten below the sheer ribband to represent the shape of the sheer strake, or *wale*. On this peapod, the wale is thicker than the planking to stiffen her up along the sheer, and to protect the ⅜-inch-thick (3/64) planking at this vulnerable spot. With the wale's shape marked on the molds, we can determine how many planks we'll need, their widths at each mold station, and from that get their approximate shapes.

Clockwise from upper left: Clamp the timbers tightly against the backbone and pin them to the ribbands....Finesse the timbers through the ribbands. Note that the ribbands are pinned to the molds; the timbers pinned to the ribbands....Start holes with a small gimlet or awl; push in the pins with needlenose pliers. Don't push the heads flush with the ribbands; you'll want to be able to get them out again.... Timbered, ribbanded hull, ready for planking. Perhaps some day I'll finish her, but to my eye, she looks pretty good as she sits.

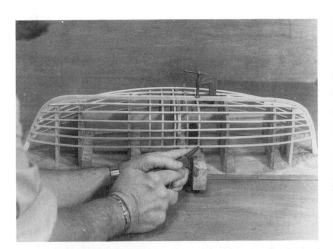

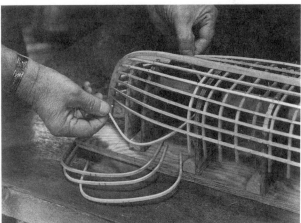

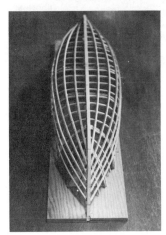

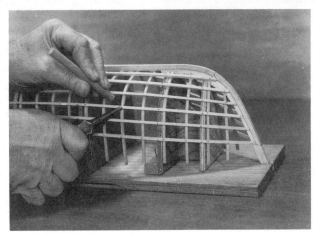

Cut a strip of paper and bend it along station 3 (the amidships mold will have the greatest distance from keel to sheer) from the underside of the wale to the keel. My model measured 33 (4¹⁄₈) inches; Phil's plans call for 11 planks below the wales. Dividing 33 by 11 means that it takes 11 planks 3 (³⁄₈) inches wide to close her in at this point on the hull. Lay that strip of paper beside your scale rule, and mark it off at 3-inch intervals. Put the paper strip back on mold 3 and mark each plank width right on the mold.

Repeat this process for the rest of the boat; you should end up with a paper strip for each mold equal to the distance between the wale and the keel. Lay out the strips flat on a piece of paper and mark their lengths. Take the key strip from station 3 and swing it between these marks until it fits, then mark off the plank widths at each station and transfer these marks back to the strips from each mold. This divides the girths and figures plank widths automatically. Put the marked strips back on the molds and transfer the plank widths.

Mine worked out like this: station 5, 2¹⁄₄ inches; station 4, 2³⁄₄ inches; station 3, 3 inches; station 2, 2⁷⁄₈ inches; station 1, 2¹⁄₂ inches. (At 1¹⁄₂-inch scale, the actual dimensions were ⁹⁄₃₂, ¹⁵⁄₃₂, ³⁄₈, ³¹⁄₆₄, and ⁵⁄₁₆ inch. See why I prefer using a scale rule for everything? Who needs dimensions like ³¹⁄₆₄?)

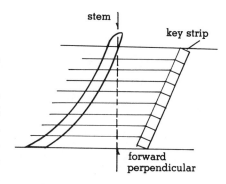

stem

key strip

forward perpendicular

Don't try to measure along the rabbet line of the stem and sternpost to determine the widths of the planks here; it won't work. Hood-end heights must be squared in from a vertical line. Square off a line where the bottom edge of the wale meets the rabbet, and extend the line down to the base. Project the rabbet line along the keel to this line, and you have the height between those points. Swing your key strip from station 3 between these marks until it fits and mark off the plank widths. For me, these worked out to be 2¹⁄₄ (⁹⁄₃₂) inches at the stem; 2 (¹⁄₄) inches at the sternpost.

Although this sounds complex, it's actually quite easy. But there's an even easier way to do it. In his book, *A Modeler's Guide to Hull Construction* (TAB Books, 1984), Richard Mansir does the job all at one crack. He takes the hull's shortest girth, usually the frame nearest the bow, marks its length on paper, and extends that into two parallel lines long enough to accommodate the rest of the odd-length strips for each mold. He cants the key strip—on which he has previously marked the plank widths—to fit between these lines and divides all the mold girths with a straightedge at one crack. That's quick, clever, and takes less time to do than to describe.

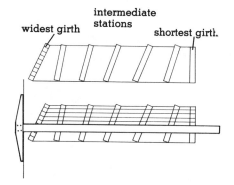

widest girth

intermediate stations

shortest girth

After you've transferred the plank widths to each mold, saw out a dozen ribbands (six for each side) a scant 1-inch square (square bends more easily), cutting them from straight-grain softwood. Starting at the sheer, put them on in pairs for every other plank, sticking them to the molds with pins. Rib-banding is really the fun part. As you apply them this random assembly of parts suddenly starts to look like a boat.

After the ribbands comes framing. This follows the proce-dure laid out earlier for framing the strip-planked model, except you'll have to worm the frames around and about the ribbands to set them in place. I made copies of the molds and prebent the frames, rather than put them in soaking wet from the ammonia tank.

To my eye the model looks great all framed out like that. I've never seen one left at that stage; they're always com-pleted. I think I'll keep her just as she is. If the urge comes, a pair of scissors and some glue can get me started planking in just a few moments.

7

The Friendship Sloop Amy R. Payson

Nautical author and sometime-*WoodenBoat* editor Peter Spectre was roaming the streets of a Canadian town one day, looking for nothing in particular, when he happened to spy a full model of a sailboat in a shop window. "Half models are nice," he thought, "but full models are better. Unlike half models, which spend their lives gathering dust on someone's wall, you can plunk them in the water and play with them. Wouldn't it be great if *WoodenBoat* offered plans for building a simple sailing model?"

Arriving back at the *WoodenBoat* mansion, Peter had no trouble convincing the editorial hierarchy of the worth of his idea, and they immediately commissioned Dave Dillion to redraw the lines of a pretty Friendship sloop, the 28-foot 10-inch *Little Hattie*, drawn originally by M. C. Erismann. And draw them Dave did, producing plans for a model with all the characteristics of the type: gaff rig with staysail and jib, clipper bow, sprung bowsprit, and a raked, elliptical transom.

The plans were drawn to a scale of 1½ inches equals 1 foot, using the *lift* or *bread-and-butter* method, a simple approach for building one curvaceous hull. *Little Hattie* was originally constructed with carvel planks over steam-bent frames, which is a lengthy and laborious task. None of that for the *Amy R. Payson!* Just cut out a bunch of wooden lifts, each representing a half-section taken parallel to the waterline, pile them up, glue them together, and carve away everything that doesn't look like a boat. That's the fun part: the more you carve, the more boat you see. As the boat's shape begins to emerge, the waterline lifts show you precisely where and how much wood to remove. It's hard to leave it alone.

I don't mean to imply that you can build a bread-and-butter model and have it sailing in a few days—no way. But I am saying that, starting right, with plans and full-size templates, you should be easily carving the hull in a couple of days. You can saw out all the lifts for the hull in about an hour. Glue them up, let them sit overnight, and start carving.

For the beginner with more ambition than skill, the construction technique used for the *Amy R.* is the easiest and most sensible approach I've seen for building an accurate model of a decked-over, round-bottom boat or ship. If you keep in mind three views of a boat: the *profile* (viewed from the side), *plan* (viewed from above), and *body* (viewed from the bow or stern), you should have no trouble. Once you have these views and this method in mind, you can build a lift-model hull, no matter what type of boat it is or who designed it.

Because my space in this book is limited, I'll address the method for building only a hull of this type, using the *Amy R.* as an example. What you learn here can be carried forward to future models, such as *Pauline*—a Maine Coast sardine carrier—that will appear in a sequel to this book. Others can be lifted directly from magazines, books, museum prints—wherever you can find plans with parallel waterlines. If you can't live without a sailing model of the *Amy R.*, you can get a complete kit from *WoodenBoat* magazine (ordering instructions in the back of this book), or, with a little ingenuity, you can cobble together her rigging and spars yourself.

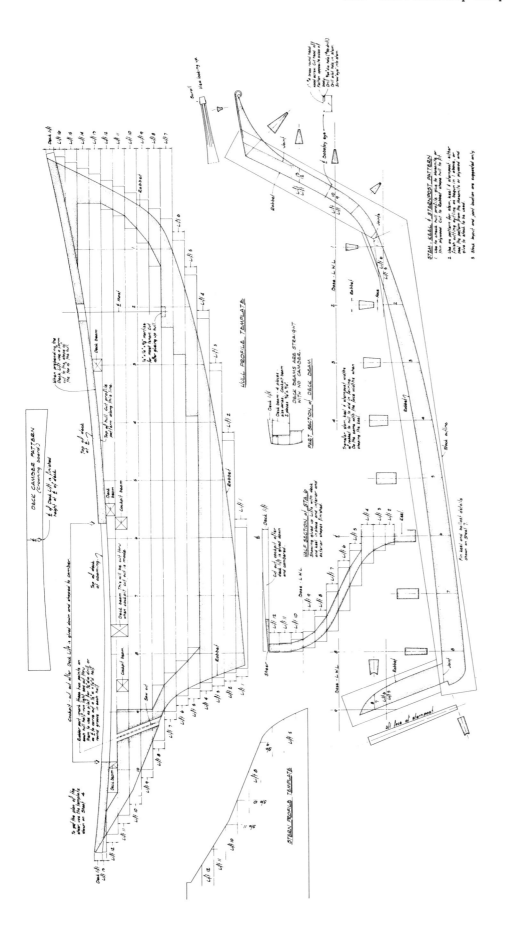

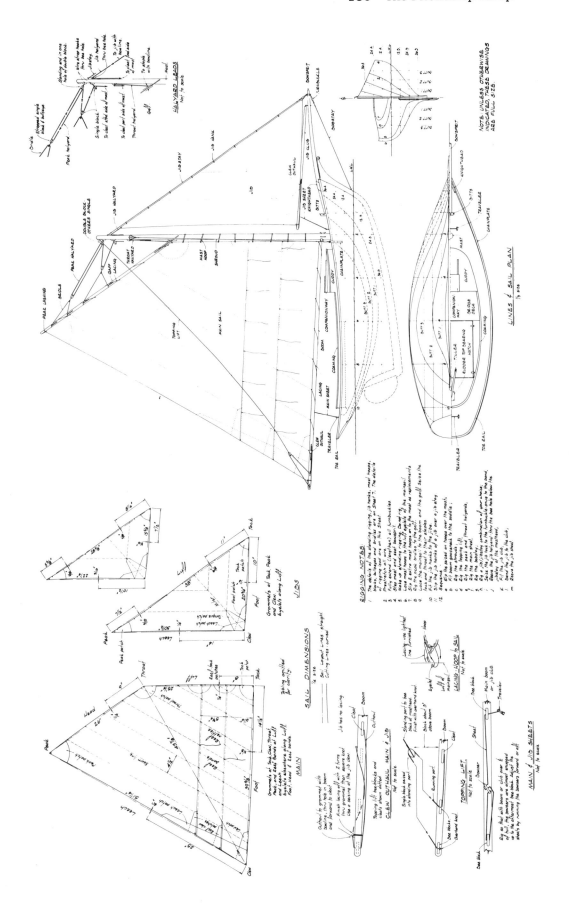

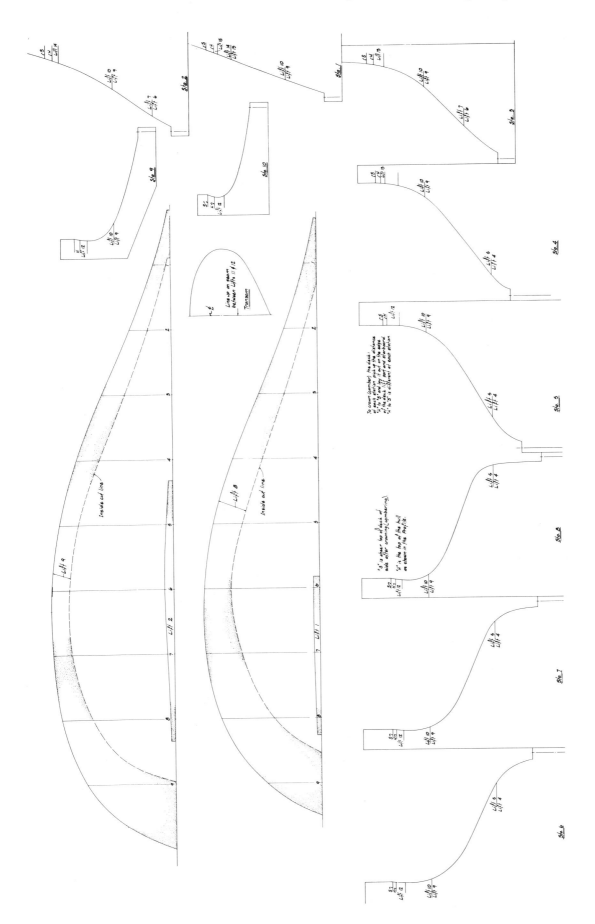

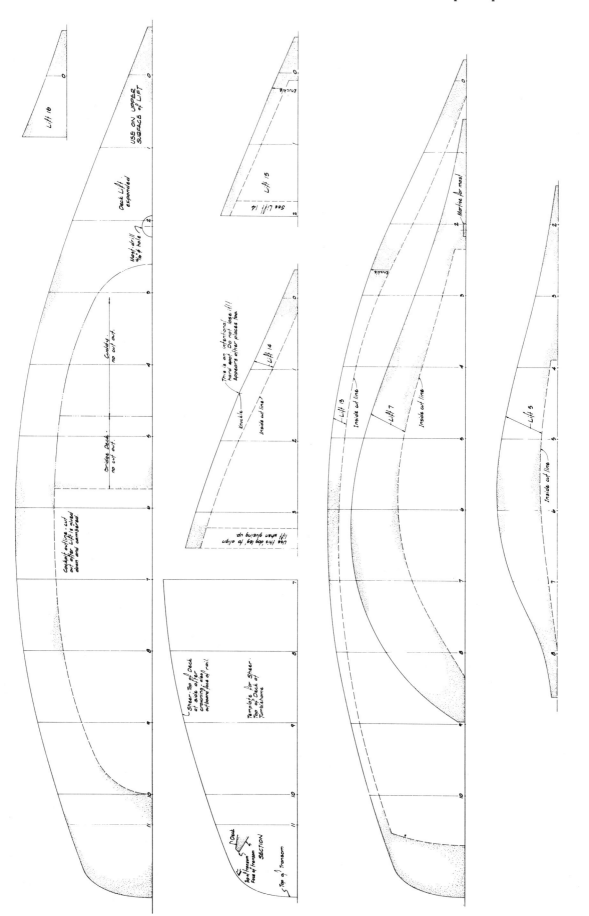

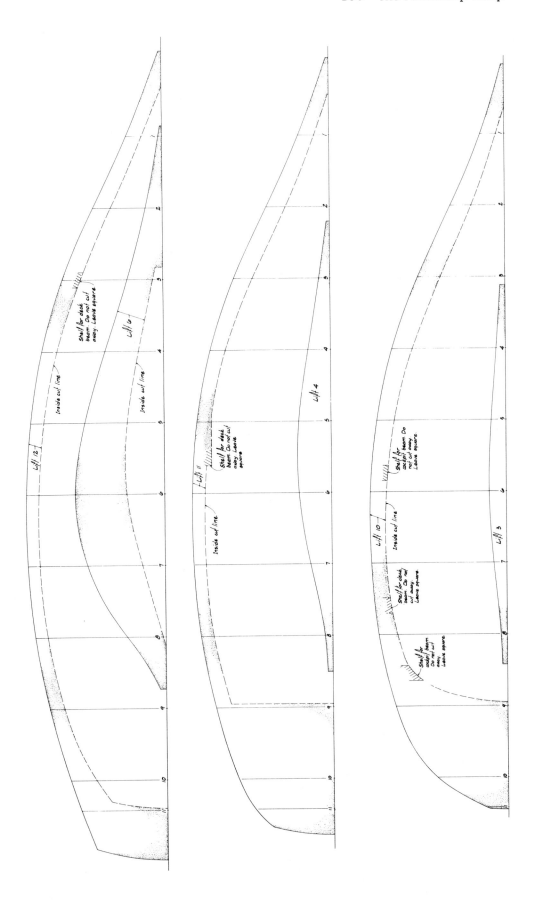

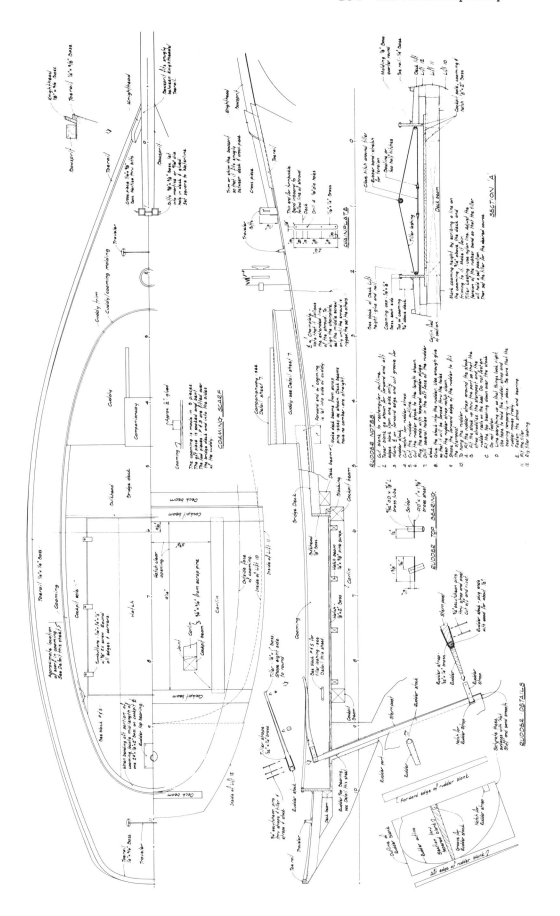

The Lift Method

Tools and Materials

The tools and materials suitable for building lift models differ little from those we have used throughout this book. For cutting out the lifts you'll need a bandsaw with a ³⁄₈-inch, skip-tooth blade, which will cut fast and produce a lot less fine sawdust to blow about your shop than the finer blades we've been using.

To rip the lift sections accurately, you'll need a good table saw—and I mean a *good* one: no pressed metal tops, no sloppy miter gauge slots. You want one with a cast metal, machine-ground table. You'll need a sharp, hollow-ground planer blade, which will give you a saw cut as smooth as if it had been planed.

If you can afford it, some kind of power scroll saw would most definitely be worth your while, especially for cutting the sharper curves in the lifts. You can live without one, but if you plan to build several lift-type models, a scroll saw will save you a lot of time.

You'll need to make long, thin, flexible sanding battens with which to fair your hull. These are most easily made from sawn-out softwood strips. Stick on sandpaper with spray adhesive (such as Blair's or 3M Spra-ment)—add a couple of handles if you've a mind to—and fair away.

This same spray adhesive can be used to make templates that are much easier to mark around for the large, complex shapes typical of hull lifts. Take a paper template that you've cut from a photocopy or tracing of the full-size plan, give it a shot of spray adhesive, stick it down on a piece of ¹⁄₈-inch tempered masonite (buy a whole sheet; you'll want it for template material), saw it out, and you've got it: instant template. In addition, these templates can be saved for posterity. Who knows, perhaps one of your kids or grandkids will want to build a model some day. Stick the templates in a case and they'll be there and waiting.

For materials, you'll need a supply of wood sawn to the thickness of the lifts. For the *Amy R.*, I used #1 kiln-dried clear pine, ³⁄₄ inch thick. This is readily available at any good lumberyard. Basswood, cedar—any fine-grain, stable wood will work as well. If your lifts work out to be a different thickness—say ¹⁄₂ inch or ⁹⁄₁₆ inch—no problem. Run some test strips through your table saw, stack them on edge right on your plans, and compare the strips' thickness to the waterlines. When you're satisfied they match, saw out the lifts.

If you're planning a model that floats, Weldwood dry powder works fine for sticking the lifts together. If your model will spend its life ashore, you can use carpenter's wood glue, such as Titebond.

For delicate work, where Weldwood or Titebond is too thick, I use "super glue," and damned carefully. Instantly bonded fingers are no fun. If it happens to you (it did to me), resist the urge to rip them apart. Instead, holler like hell for your spouse to dump fingernail polish remover on your stuck fingers. After that experience, any tiny parts that needed gluing I impaled on a pin.

Cut out the paper patterns for the half-section lifts and the body sections, cutting well outside the lines. Leave the insides of the lifts solid for now; we don't want the paper templates to edge set.

Getting Started

Stick each roughly-cut paper pattern down on masonite with spray adhesive, and saw out the templates on your bandsaw as accurately as possible. Trace their shape onto your lift stock and cut out the lifts. Set the body section templates aside for now; we'll use them to check the hull's shape later, as we carve.

Square the station lines all around the lifts. Use one amidships station line as a reference point to align the lifts when you stack them. Pair each half-lift with its mate on a flat surface to ensure that they're identical. If they aren't, make them so, using a block plane, spokeshave, or rasp—whatever it takes.

The *Amy R.*, designed from the start to be a sailing model, was drawn with hollow lifts. When I built the sardine carrier *Pauline,* I wanted a hollow hull so I could have removable hatch covers looking down into a real fish hold. I had to figure out how to hollow the lifts myself or pay a draftsman. It ended up being easier than I could believe. I cut out all the lifts solid (and left the bottom lifts that way), stacked them on edge like a deck of cards, with their sections aligned, then marked the shape of one from its neighbor. I offset them by about an inch so there would be enough wood left in the hull after carving to shape. Unbelievably easy. I did it by eye; no math involved.

With the lifts cut out, build an L-shaped jig to glue up each half of the hull. This should be a little wider than half the beam, a little higher than the greatest depth, and a good 6 or 8 inches longer than the hull. For the *Amy R.*, that worked out to be 12 inches high, 8 inches wide, and 48 inches long. This jig must be perfectly square; brace it well to keep it that way. Square off two lines amidships—one plumb on the backboard, the other squared from it on the base. Staple waxed paper over the jig to keep the lifts from sticking to it.

Think of buttering slices of bread as you glue up each half-hull, a few lifts at a time, working from the top lift toward the bottom. As you add each lift, check its centerline against the jig's centerline with a square. If the lifts won't sit still, drive brads into them through the backboard. Clamp or weight the lifts as the glue sets. If your hull is built up higher at the bow with half-length lifts, as is the *Amy R.*, trig up under the stern with temporary lifts (don't glue them) of a matching thickness.

While the glue is drying on the last half-hull, cut out a paper pattern for the hull profile, glue it to masonite, and cut it out. Lay it on the flat side of a half-hull, align the lift lines from the plans with the stacked layers, and trace around the template. This gives you the exact profile shape of the planked hull right to a cat's whisker.

Saw out the profile on your bandsaw (you can use a coping saw and a block plane), cutting 90 degrees to the line, except back aft. Here, you'll want to cut to the line at a shallow angle to keep from removing too much wood. Trace the shape

Bread and Butter

Clockwise from upper left: Cut out the paper patterns for the lifts and body sections....Transfer the body sections...and the lifts to thin masonite, stiff cardboard, etc. Saw out the templates, trace them onto your lift stock, and saw out the lifts....Pair each lift with its mate on a flat surface; they must be identical.

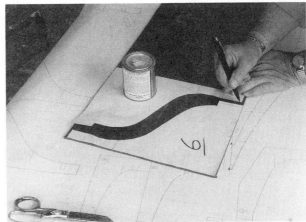

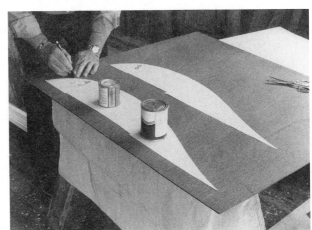

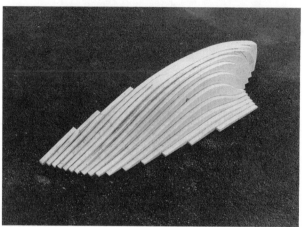 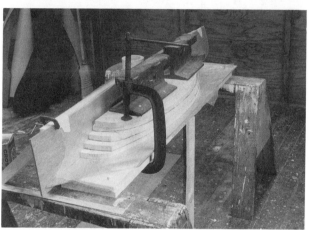

of the trimmed half-hull on the untrimmed hull and cut it to match.

Lay the profile template back on the half-hull, hang a combination square over its edge, and square off the sheer inside the hull. Make closely spaced pencil dots where the square touches the hull. You won't need a batten to sweep in the line; the pencil marks will work fine. Repeat the process for the other half-hull.

Sawing the sheer is tricky. A model with this many curves wants to roll all over your bandsaw table, making it most difficult to cut. Nevertheless, faced with the thought of doing it by hand, I used my bandsaw. I cocked the table (just as I did when sawing out the plug for the dory in Chapter 3) so the blade would miss the hidden line by a good margin. Don't do this unless you trust your bandsawing skills completely. Do it by hand.

Clockwise from upper left: Build a jig, making it a perfect and well-braced right angle. Draw on a centerline. Cover the jig with waxed paper....Stack and glue the lifts, a few at a time. Square them from the centerline. Fasten them to the jig temporarily with finishing nails....Clamp and weight the lifts while the glue dries....A completed half-hull. Note the extra lifts at the bow for the sheer.

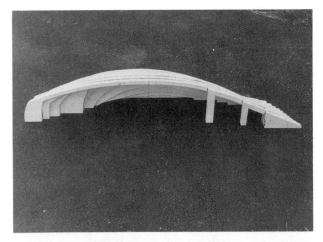

With the sheer of both half-hulls cut roughly to shape, glue the two halves together, matching the lift lines, station lines, and profiles exactly. Clamp the hull together with blocks and wedges, bar clamps, a Spanish windlass—whatever it takes.

When the glue dries, turn the hulls rightside up and support them securely. Tack sandpaper to a long, flat board and fair the sheer lines, working square across, not diagonally, until you're down to the marked sheer line. The deck goes on next, and is cambered athwartships with a crowning board. The *Amy R.*'s crowning board is shown on the plans. If you're working from different plans, refer back to Chapter 6, where we made one to crown the breasthooks and gunwales for the peapod.

The *Amy R.*'s deck was made from 1/2-inch pine, soaked and let dry over a form cut to the deck's sheer. Cut out a paper pattern for the deck, trace it onto the crowned deck stock, and

Clockwise from upper left: Glue up the other half-hull. Make sure the two halves come out exactly alike....Scrape off the excess glue, and plane and sand the back of the completed half-hull perfectly flat....If you're building a sailing model and you want to save weight, or if you're just excessively neat, chisel and plane off the corners between lifts....Cut out a profile pattern, glue it to masonite, lay it on one half-hull (align it with the lift lines), and trace the profile shape.

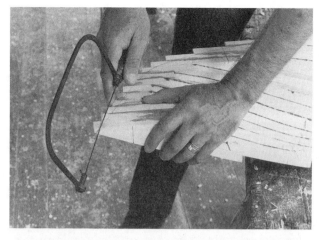

saw it out. Make wide decks in two halves joined down the centerline, just as we did for the hulls.

Glue deck beams into the hull where indicated, or around any openings you might plan to cut through the deck, and glue down the deck to the beams and to the sheer. Check the sheer line by measuring the distance from the uppermost station line to the top of the sheer. Make tick marks at each point, connect them with a batten, and fair the sheer with sandpaper mounted on a block.

Clockwise from upper left: Trim the profile to the line with a coping saw and block plane. If you're confident of your abilities, save yourself some time and use a bandsaw....Trim reverse-curve sections, such as around the stern, at an angle to avoid removing too much wood. Finish with a block plane.... Trace the shape of the completed half-hull onto its mate and trim it to match.... Clamp the profile template to one half-hull and transfer the sheer with a combination square and pencil, making closely spaced dots along the sheer.

As you know by now, I'm a little on the lazy side, and I like to get a job done by taking the most direct approach possible. So when I was faced with the job of knocking all those square corners off the lifts to get started carving the hull, I grabbed my electric block plane and mowed down the excess wood in about 20 minutes. I'm not saying you should use my method; there is nothing wrong with taking your time—if you have it. If you'd rather do the whole job with hand tools, go to it.

Once you get the corners off, work the hull down with a hand block plane, wood rasps, spokeshave, and sandpaper. The hardest part to carve is around the tuck—the transition

Carving the Hull

Clockwise from upper left: Connect the dots from the combination square with a batten; saw both half-hulls roughly to the line....Match the lift lines, station lines, and profiles, and glue the two halves together....When the glue dries, fair the sheer to the lines with spokeshave, blockplane, and sandpaper mounted on a block, working square across the model....Fit and glue in place any deck beams and the deck lift.

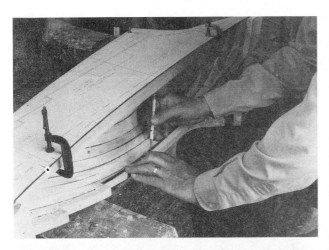

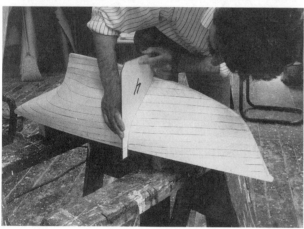

from the more-or-less vertical keel to deadrise near the stern post. Re-mark any station lines you obliterate; you'll need them to check the hull's contours.

When the waterlines start blending in to one another, start checking at each station line with the body section templates. Hold these at right angles to the hull at their proper station and sight toward them along the hull. Fit each body section as closely as you can.

When you're satisfied with the contour at each station, it's time to fair the hull, using thin, flexible battens with sandpaper stuck to them. Dust a batten with a little carpenter's chalk and try it along the hull; this will pick up humps and hollows quickly. Continue hand sanding until the hull is perfectly fair and smooth.

Clockwise from upper left: Check the sheer line by measuring from the uppermost lift up to the sheer, as indicated on the plans. Make a tick mark at each station and connect the dots with a batten....Knock off the corners with a plane, rasp, spokeshave, whatever. I used a power block plane. Hollow areas of the hull are best done with a fishtail gouge....When you have the corners roughed off, set your plane for a finer cut and start paring to the glue lines, cutting with the grain and being careful not to take off too much wood....Check the hull's shape at each station with the body section templates. Fair the hull with sandpaper mounted on a long, flexible block of wood.

The addition of the backbone, consisting of the keel, stem, and sternpost, finishes the hull. Cut out the patterns, templates, and parts—in the *Amy R.*'s case, from ³/₄-inch pine—just as we've done right along. Glue them together on waxed paper lying directly on the plans.

Draw a centerline on the backbone to aid establishing its correct shape. Make tick marks along its length to establish the widths at various points, and connect them with a flexible batten.

Try the backbone in place on the hull, sighting along its length for unfair spots. If the backbone fits too tightly, shave a bit off the hull. It should drop into place on the hull without forcing. When you achieve this, you're as close to perfection

Finishing the Hull

Clockwise from upper left: Assemble the backbone components...and strike a centerline on the finished product. Glue it in place on the hull....Cut out any openings in the hull. Here, Spectre is cutting out the cockpit....The cockpit cut out and framed, the mast stepped, and the billethead glued on.

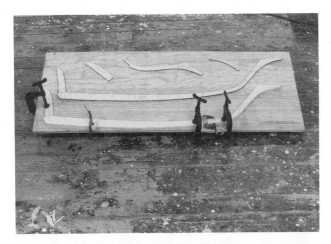

and to fidelity to the architect's lines as you're likely to get. Add scribed deck planking, deckhouses and furniture, mast and rigging, and a good paint job, and you have a model indistinguishable from one planked up over molds—and a lot less work.

Am I excited about this simplified, hollow-lift method of model-building? You bet! It's opened up a whole new way of boatbuilding for me.

Just for the fun of it, and to prove to myself how well this basic concept works to produce an accurate model from minimal information, I recently tackled the job of building a model of the sardine carrier *Pauline.* Back in the Forties, in the heyday of the Maine herring-fishing industry, Newbert and Wallace Shipyard, of Thomaston, Maine, built a fleet of these beautiful, seagoing boats, with their narrow beam and canoe sterns, ranging from 70 feet to the *Pauline's* 83 feet on deck. They were common sights all along the coast of Maine, nosing in and out of remote coves, calling at weirs and stop seines for

Clockwise from upper left: Glue up lifts for the cuddy or any deckhouses.... Clamp the coaming (soaked to make it bend easily) around forms...and glue it in place....The *Amy R. Payson,* ready for a sail in Penobscot Bay.

Over the Horizon

loads of herring destined for the sardine plants at Rockland, Boothbay, or Belfast.

Like many things, the herring industry isn't what it used to be. I had heard the *Pauline* was hauled out in Rockland for conversion into a passenger-carrying cruise boat. When I found her, she was stripped to the deck, her pilothouse lying on the ground, and her two masts beside it in a tangle of rigging. She was a perfect candidate. As luck would have it, her new owners, Captains Ken and Ellen Barnes, had *Pauline's* lines drawn up by Wiscasset naval architects Woodin and Marean. Everyone was interested in the modelbuilding project, and they gave me a copy of her lines. Drawn at ³/₈ inch equals 1 foot, it would be a new challenge working in a smaller scale. So would crawling all over her with a tape measure, filling in the blanks.

As it turned out, working in ³/₈-inch scale wasn't as tough as I thought. I just rolled the scale rule over to the proper scale. In some respects it was even easier than larger scale. I could order all of *Pauline's* hardware—her shaft, wheel, chocks, and mushroom ventilators—right from Bluejacket Shipcrafters.

Was all that work worth it? My eyes say yes, as I look at her sitting in my shop vise, ready for her final coat of paint. In fact I'm already thinking about my next model—another sardine carrier. For this one, the *William Underwood*, I have the complete set of original builder's plans from Eldredge McInnis, which means I won't be running back and forth to Rockland with a tape measure. And I'll build her by the same lift method. I see no point in going to all that work lining off planking, then painting over it. Some would, and to each his own.

This lift method does work, and works well. If you have a profile, plan view, and body sections, you can work them together this simple way and build a model from scratch to be proud of. Think about it, tackle one, and have fun.

Left to right: The *Pauline,* all rigged and ready to go....The *Pauline's* designer and builder Roy Wallace and a disinterested observer.

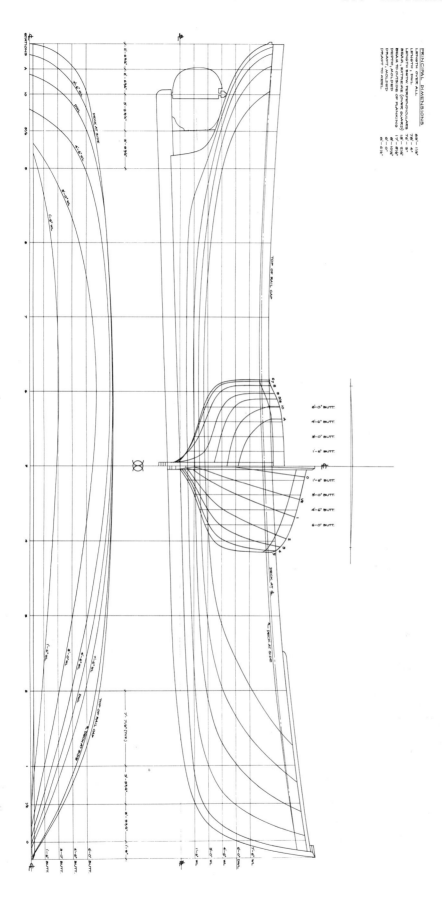

Reflections

As I mentioned in the first part of this book, most of what I do has been by inspiration. As I look back on quite a few years of fooling around with boats, I could add *luck* to that as well. Luck has played a good part in shaping my life—still does. Luck led me into an association with Phil Bolger after I wrote telling him that I was taken with his design for the Gloucester Light Dory. Luck led Peter Spectre into my shop, lugging a bunch of plans for this Friendship sloop model; luck even led me to build it.

It was early spring, and I was heading for the water and real boats. When I agreed initially, I had thought it would be a winter project. When Peter said it was a "now" project, I said no thanks. But a week later Peter asked, "What if I can find you some help?" He waited a bit then said, "What if I help you?" I thought for a moment and said, "OK, let's do it." I came that close to not building the model at all. Looking back I can see I would have cheated myself out of both a valuable learning experience and an enjoyable job. Just luck.

Building the *Amy R.* led me down the path toward model-building. I realized there was little on the market other than full-rigged ships or kits. I have nothing against either, but it did

The sardine carrier *Pauline*.

occur to me that, because it's likely the unskilled outnumber the skilled, there should be more to offer them. Hence this book.

For my money, there are enough models of full-rigged ships already, and enough people to write about them. I want to preserve in miniature the simple working craft—tugboats, draggers, lobsterboats, shrimpers—with which I am most familiar, and which are most pleasing to my eye.

Those—and the lift method—will be the subject of my next book.

Catch you later.

Enlarging Plans

Here's a brief introduction to a very small part of the mystic skill of *lofting*—drawing a curvaceous boat full size in three dimensions from cryptic instructions or smaller plans. In its simplest form, it's much easier than you would imagine.

Using these methods, you can enlarge any of the chine-type boats in this book to full model size. Round-bottom boats are a little more complicated, but I'll give you a thumbnail sketch of the procedure; you should be able to puzzle out the rest. After all, your only investment is a little time, pencil lead, and paper. If you want to know how to *really* loft, check out the lofting section of a good boatbuilding text, such as *Boatbuilding Manual*, by Robert M. Steward (IMP, 1987); *Lofting*, by Allan H. Vaitses (IMP, 1980); or *Boatbuilding*, by Howard I. Chapelle, (W.W. Norton, 1969).

You'll need:

Materials Needed:

- a smooth wooden work surface that you don't mind perforating profusely, a good foot larger in all dimensions than the boat's final size. A sheet of smooth-sanded plywood painted white works well
- tracing paper or Mylar (check art supply stores)
- sharp carpenter's pencils and an eraser
- steel measuring tape
- scale rule
- framing square
- a quantity of straight-grain battens, ranging from about 1/8-inch to 3/8-inch square, at least a foot longer than your boat
- a quantity of straight-grain, 1/2-inch-square sticks with genuinely square ends
- a quantity of long steel pins or brads

Prepare your drawing board by gluing on a dead-straight bottom batten. You'll rest your framing square on this when you erect the *perpendiculars*—accurately spaced lines running at right angles to the bottom batten, or *baseline*, along which the boat's heights are measured. Pin your drawing paper down with its bottom butted firmly against the bottom batten.

With your scale rule flopped to the scale of choice, make a mark to locate each *station line* (the spacing for which will be given in most boat plans) along the bottom batten. Example: the station lines might be spaced, reading in feet, inches, and eighths from the aft perpendicular forward, 2,2,2; 2,6,0; 2,6,0; 2,6,0; 2,6,0; 2,8,2. In other words, 2 feet, 2 inches, and 2/8 inch, etc. Make a tick mark on the bottom batten at the proper intervals. Set your framing square on the bottom batten and erect a perpendicular line at each station. Label each one clearly (station 1, etc.).

For simple boats, that's all the preliminary layout work you'll need. For more complicated round-bottom boats you'll need to draw a *grid,* which consists of *waterlines,* parallel to and spaced accurately from the baseline on the profile view, and *buttock lines,* parallel to and spaced accurately from the centerline on the plan view (looking down). These dimensions will be on the plans or in the table of offsets. Label these as well.

Now let's draw our boat's *profile.* Find the baseline on your plans. Note the measurement for height given above the baseline (either on the plans or in the table of offsets) for the bow. Transfer this measurement to the forward perpendicular, measuring up from the baseline with your scale rule. Push in a pin at the exact spot.

Repeat the process for each of the station lines and we're ready to sweep in the sheer (or bottom, if the boat's drawn

A typical lines plan for a simple, round-bottom boat. Reproduced from *Boatbuilding Manual* (IMP, 1987); courtesy Robert Steward.

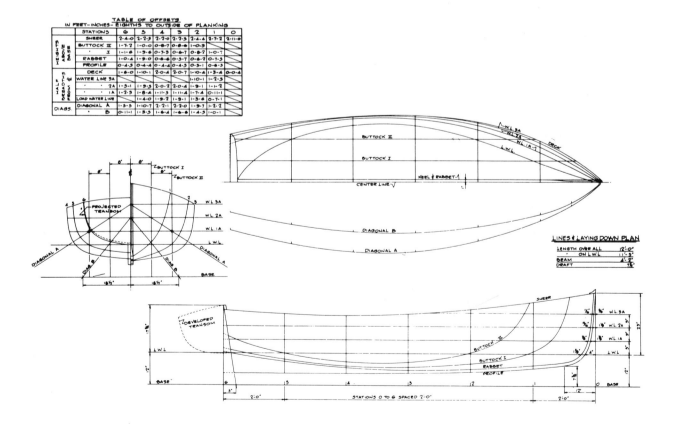

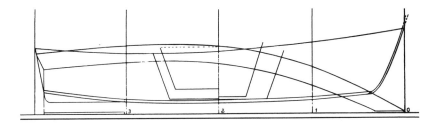

Lofting a simple flat-bottom boat, with the profile, plan view, and body section superimposed. Courtesy Allan H. Vaitses.

upside down from the baseline). Remember the connect-the-dots exercise in *My Weekly Reader?* That's just how you draw in these sweeping lines, only we use a *batten* to fair the curves.

Bend one of your battens around the pins (DON'T stick pins through the battens; you're guaranteed an unfair curve and a ruined batten), letting it run well off the board. Stick other pins above or below the batten as needed so it stays in place.

Stick your head right down at batten level and sight along it. Any humps, hollows, or unfair spots? If so, move the pins around very slightly until the batten is perfectly fair. Designers sometimes make drafting errors in taking offsets; your fairing process takes these out.

Sharpen a carpenter's pencil to a fine chisel point and draw in the curve along the batten, being careful not to push it unfair. Pull the pins and remove the batten and your first line's drawn for the profile.

Follow the same connect-the-dots procedure for the other profile lines. For a flat-bottom boat, there should be only the sheer and chine, transom and stem. A V-bottom boat will have a bottom line as well as a chine line; a multi-chine boat would have a line for each chine. Round-bottom boats have buttock lines (see the accompanying illustration).

A rounded stem is drawn much the same way as the sheer line: tick off the heights above the baseline; tick off the distances back from the forward perpendicular; insert pins and connect the dots. You'll need a very supple batten to bend in a curved bow.

Now, superimposed on the profile drawing, draw the plan (or half-breadth) view, just as you did the profile, using the baseline as the half-breadth centerline. First draw the keel, often just a line parallel to the centerline. Next draw the deck line, using pins and battens, just as you did for the sheer line on the profile. Repeat the process for the chine. Round-bottom boats will have the waterlines drawn in.

Now you have the full-size faired top view superimposed on the full-size faired side view, and you're ready to pick up the dimensions directly from here to draw the body plan.

Pin another piece of tracing paper directly over the plan and profile views. Erect a perpendicular on this—the *center-*

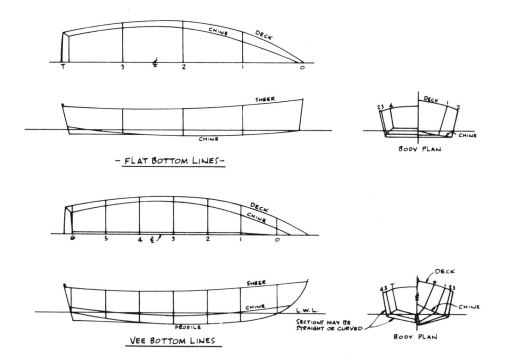

- FLAT BOTTOM LINES -

VEE BOTTOM LINES

line—over the plan and profile's amidships station. If the plan you're enlarging has buttock lines and waterlines, draw these in too, tracing them from the profile and half-breadth views. These must match exactly if the body plan is to be accurate.

We'll draw one-half of the body section at a time. The right-hand side of the drawing will be the boat's port side looking aft; the left-hand side will be the port side looking forward. Fasten a straight batten along the centerline to butt your ruler against, leaving the batten to the left of the line.

Assume for the moment that we're working with a flat-bottom boat. Lay one of your ½-inch-square battens—more commonly called a *pickup stick* or *story pole*—on station 1, butted up tight against the bottom batten. Mark where each of the lines you drew on the profile and plan crosses the station line and label it. Example: HT-B (for height, bottom); HB-B (for half-breadth, bottom); HB-S (for half-breadth, sheer), HT-S (for height, sheer), etc. Mark a station on each of the pickup stick's four sides, being sure to mark the station number on the proper side.

Butt your pickup stick against the center and bottom battens and push in a pin at the HT-B mark. Slide the pickup stick out parallel to the center batten, a little farther than you estimate the bottom's half-width to be, and push in another pin at the HT-B mark. You've got the bottom's height above the baseline.

Now swing the pickup stick around to rest on the pins, butt its end against the center batten, and push in a pin at the HB-B

Straight-sectioned boats have simple lines, and are therefore easier to loft. Courtesy Robert Steward.

mark. You've got the bottom's width from the centerline. Draw a line along the batten to represent the bottom and pull the first two pins. Leave the last pin where it is; we'll use it to draw the sides.

Repeat this same process for the sheer line, again leaving the last pin in place. Lay a straightedge between the bottom pin and the sheer pin, draw the line, and there's your first mold section drawn. Leave the sheer and bottom pins in place. Repeat the process for each station back to amidships.

Now relocate the center batten to the right side of the centerline and repeat the process for the other set of body sections. There's your half sections, all ready to trace over, cut out, and make molds. It isn't absolutely necessary, but you can sweep in the sheer and bottom lines, just the way you did in the profile and plan views, using battens bent around the pins at the bottom and sheer lines.

V-bottom boats are only slightly more complex. Here you need to push in pins at the bottom along the keel, at the chine, and at the sheer. Connect the dots exactly the same way.

Round-bottom boats are a slightly different kettle of fish— not a completely new recipe for chowder, just a few more ingredients. These are the buttock lines, waterlines, and diagonals (diagonals help to keep the body sections' curved lines accurate), and are measured, ticked off, faired, battened, pickup sticked, and drawn in, just as described earlier. Instead of connecting the body section dots with straightedges, however, as we did for flat- and V-bottom boats, you sweep in the lines using flexible battens.

There it is in a nutshell: If you sit down with paper, pencil, battens, and a handful of pins, you'll be surprised how quickly you pick it up.

Plans for boats in this book:
H.H. Payson & Co.
Pleasant Beach Rd.
South Thomaston, ME 04858
(A study packet of 25 boat plans is available for $5 postpaid.)

Kit for Amy R. Payson *and other models:*
WoodenBoat
PO Box 78
Brooklin, ME 04616

Modeling supplies, tools, and materials of all kinds:
Micro-Mark
340 Snyder Ave.
Berkeley Heights, NJ 07922

Metal fittings, kits, plans, supplies:
Bluejacket Shipcrafters
Castine, ME 04421

Japan dryer, fiberglassing supplies:
Hamiltons Marine, Inc.
PO Box 227
Searsport, ME 04974

Brass pins:
Newark Dressmaker Supply
6473 Ruch Road
PO Box 2448
Lehigh Valley, PA 18001

Custom clamp makers:
R. Ullom Co.
Orwell, VT 05760

Basswood:
A.E. Sampson & Son
PO Box 1010
Warren, ME 04864

Aft. Toward the stern.

After. Closer to the stern.

Amidships. In the middle portion of a boat. As an adjective, "midships."

Athwartships. Running across the hull. As an adjective, "thwartships."

Baseline. A line, usually parallel to the waterline, drawn on boat plans and used as a reference for all vertical measurements when lofting the lines of a hull.

Batten. A thin, flat length of wood that can be sprung through a series of reference points and thereby used to determine and draw a fair curve through the points.

Bevel. An angle cut along the edge of a timber or across its end to produce an exact fit between parts of a hull.

Bilge. The lower internal region of a hull, or (often as "turn of the bilge") the region of maximum curvature between the bottom and sides in a cross-sectional view of a round-bottomed boat.

Breasthook. A thwartship structural member near the stem.

Bulkhead. A thwartship panel dividing a hull into sections. Equivalent to a frame mold in an Instant Boat.

Butt. To join end-to-end or edge-to-edge. As a noun, a butt strap or butt block fastened across such a joint to hold the two elements together. Also, the lower end of a mast.

Carvel Planking. A method of planking in which the strakes or planks are fastened to the frames of a hull edge to edge.

Centerboard. A short, hinged, retractable keel used to reduce leeway in a sailboat. It is raised and lowered through a watertight case, or trunk.

Centerline. On boat plans, a line dividing a hull into two identical fore-and-aft sections, and used as a base for establishing thwartship measurements when lofting. Also, a vertical line on thwartship members used to align them during assembly.

Chine. A longitudinal joint where panel edges meet in a hull constructed of a sheet material such as plywood. Most commonly, the joint between sides and bottom in a flat- or V-bottom boat.

Chine Log. A reinforcing strip of wood along the inside or outside of a chine, to which the joining panels are fastened.

Cleat. A fitting to which a line can be made fast. Any short length of small dimensional lumber used for miscellaneous framing needs.

Clew. The lower, aftermost corner of a sail.

Cringle. A reinforced aperture in a sail, such as a metal grommet, through which a line can be passed.

Deadrise. The upward slant of the bottom of a hull to the chine in a V-bottom hull, or from the keel to the turn of the bilge in a round-bottom hull.

Dory. A flat-bottomed craft that has flaring sides and a narrow stern. It is capable of carrying heavy loads but is very tender when light.

Double-ended. Having a sharp end at both bow and stern (e.g., a canoe or a peapod).

Edge-nailed. A method of planking in which successive narrow strakes, usually square or nearly so, are fastened together with nails and generally glued as well.

Edge-set. In a carvel-planked boat, to drive one plank down forcibly to meet the plank below despite irregularities in the planks.

Face. The flat, broad surface of a board or timber.

Fair. Said of a graceful curve that changes gradually and has no bumps, hollows, or flat places. Used also as a verb.

Flare. The outward angle of a boat's sides between waterline and sheer when viewed in cross section.

Flush. Even or level with, not protruding.

Foot. The bottom edge of a sail. Also, the butt of a mast.

Frame or Frame Mold. A thwartship member to which planking is fastened.

Framing Piece. A strengthening member fastened to the edge of a bulkhead or transom to add rigidity.

Freeboard. At any given point along a hull, the height of the sheer above the waterline.

Gaff. The spar to which the head of a gaff sail is lashed. It has a set of jaws that run up or down the mast when the sail is hoisted or lowered.

Gaff-headed. Describing a sailing rig such as *Bobcat* has, consisting of a quadrilateral fore-and-aft sail fitted with a gaff.

Garboard. In a carvel-planked boat, the plank next to the keel, either port or starboard.

Grommet. A round, metal eyelet or a ring of rope sewn into a sail or other piece of cloth.

Gudgeon. A metal eye or other aperture installed on the keel, skeg, or transom of a boat, into which the rudder pintles fit when the rudder is shipped or installed.

Gunwale. The longitudinal strengthening strip that runs along the sheer of a hull from bow to stern. (Pronounced gunn'l)

Gusset. A stiffening bracket fastened to any two structural members where they meet at an angle near 90 degrees.

Halyard. The line, reeved through a block or similar device, with which the sail is raised.

Head. The top corner of a jibheaded sail or the top edge of a quadrilateral sail. In a gaff rig, the head of the sail is attached to the gaff.

Heel. The foot or butt of the mast or the end of a frame at the keel. As a verb, the tendency of a sailboat to lean from the vertical in response to the pressure of the wind on the sails.

Inboard. Within the limits of the hull area.

Jaws. A U-shaped fitting on the inboard end of a boom or gaff that allows the spar to swing around the mast.

Jig. A wooden structure on a fixed base on which the parts of a boat can be assembled. A jig determines the shape of the part.

Keel. The main structural member and longitudinal backbone of a hull; it usually extends below the hull to help keep the boat on a heading and reduce leeway.

Knee. A strengthening timber that is fastened to two angled members and distributes stress to both.

Lapstrake. A method of planking in which each strake slightly overlaps the one below it, giving the appearance of clapboards.

Leech. The after edge of a fore-and-aft sail.

Limber Holes. Apertures in bulkheads that allow water in the bilge to move from one section of the hull to another.

Lofting. The process of laying out the patterns of the parts of a hull full size, working from plans drawn to scale.

Luff. As a noun, the forward edge of a fore-and-aft sail. As a verb, to head up into the wind so much that the forward edge of the sail begins to shake.

Mast. The vertical spar that is the main support column of the sailing rig.

Mast Partner. A transverse member located at a height just below the sheerline of a boat, through which the mast passes to acquire steadiness and bearing.

Mold. A pattern of a transverse section of a hull, set up in construction but removed when the hull nears completion. A frame mold acts as a mold but remains in the finished hull.

Offsets. A table of measurements from the baseline and centerline that establish points defining the shape of a hull. Offsets are used to loft and lay down the lines of a boat full size.

Outboard. Outside the limits of the hull, or in a direction away from the centerline.

Peak. In a sprit or gaff sail, the after upper corner of the quadrilateral.

Pintle. A vertical pin or rod used to hang or hinge a rudder. Pintles are attached to the forward or leading edge of the rudder and slide into gudgeons fixed to the stern of a boat. (See Gudgeon.)

Prebore. To bore a hole in wood that a nail or other fastening will be driven into. Preboring reduces the danger of breaking out or splitting. The holes should be slightly smaller than the wire diameter of the shank of the fastening.

Quarter. One of the two outboard quadrants of a boat's stern.

Rabbet. A beveled recess cut into the stem to receive the forward, or hood, ends of the planking and into the keel to receive the lower edge of the garboard strake.

Rake. A departure from the vertical of any member of a boat, such as the stem, transom, or mast.

Run. The curve of the bottom of a hull as it rises from a point near amidships toward the stern. If the rise is gentle, with little rocker, the boat is said to have a flat run.

Scarf. As a verb, to glue two beveled pieces of wood end to end or edge to edge; beveling allows the pieces to overlap without an increase in thickness. As a noun, describes a joint so made.

Seam. The joint between two planks or strakes, rendered watertight by caulking.

Seize. To bind together; or, to put a stopper on a line. Line for seizing is always smaller and lighter than the line to which it is applied.

Sheer. The uppermost line of a hull viewed in profile, also called the sheerline. The top plank, or strake, on a hull is the sheerstrake.

Sheet. A line used to control the positioning of a sail in relation to the wind. On a sail attached to a boom, the sheet is made fast to the boom near its outboard end; on a loose-footed sail, it is attached to the clew.

Shim. To wedge up or fill out with thin sheets of metal or wood.

Shutter. The strake that closes in a hull that has been planked both up from the keel and down from the sheer.

Snotter. A line that bears on or near the butt of a sprit to maintain its thrust against either the clew of a jibheaded sail or the peak of a quadrilateral sail.

Spanish Windlass. A length of line looped around the planks or side panels of a hull to pull them into place, usually by means of a lever that twists the line and constricts the loop. In action it resembles a tourniquet.

Spar. Any timber (mast, boom, gaff, or sprit) used to support a sailing rig.

Spile. To determine and scribe a line that defines the shape of any element in a hull so that it will exactly fit an adjoining element as required. Most frequently, to transfer the shape of the upper edge of a plank or strake onto the bottom edge of the plank to be fastened immediately above it.

Sprit. A spar used to set a spritsail by extending the clew of a triangular sail or the peak of a quadrilateral sail.

Spritsail. Any sail set by means of a sprit.

Stem. The foremost vertical or nearly vertical structural member of a boat's hull; sometimes called a cutwater.

Stemcap. External fairing piece that overlays the planking joint at the stem.

Strake. A single unit of the planking that closes in a boat's hull.

Tack. The forward lower corner of any fore-and-aft sail.

Template. A pattern cut from wood, metal, or paper and used to scribe lines on building stock.

Throat. The forward upper corner of a quadrilateral fore-and-aft sail.

Thwart. A transverse member, often a seat for crew or passengers.

Transom. The after face of the stern of a boat; often, the entire stern.

Trunk. A narrow boxlike structure, open to the sea at the bottom of the boat, through which a centerboard or daggerboard can be lowered to extend below the bottom; also called a case.

Tumblehome. The inward curve of the upper sides of a hull toward the centerline.

V-bottom Boat. A chine boat whose deadrise is flat between the keel and the chine; sometimes called a deadrise boat.

Wale. The strip of planking running beneath the gunwale, parallel to the sheer.

Waterline. Any horizontal line on a boat's profile generated by a plane parallel to the surface of the water. The LWL, load waterline, is the upper limit of a boat's draft under normal conditions with the designed load.

Aft perpendicular. *See* A.P.
Amy R. Payson, 147–164, 167
A.P., 116
Architect's scale rule, 18, 169

Backbone assembly, 62, 67, 117–119,
    163–164
Bandsaw, xv, 3, 138, 155
Barnes, Ken and Ellen, 165
Baseline, 28, 169
Bates, Fred, 121
Bearding line, 119
Betts, Jim, 94
Bevel gauge, 20
Bilge panels, 67–68, 77–83, 89–90
Bluejacket Shipcrafters, 165, 174
Boatbuilding in Your Own Backyard
    (Rabl), 135
Bobcat, 57–72, 76
Body view, 148, 162, 171–173
Bolger, Phil, 37, 52, 57, 75, 102, 167
Boottop, 97
Bottom planking, 21–22, 48–50, 77–83
Bowsaw, 3
Bow seat, 90–91
Brass pins, xvi–xvii
Bread-and-butter method. *See* Lift
    method
Bread-and-butter models, 147–165
Breasthooks, 131–134
Brewer, Ted, 94
Building base, 109–117, 123
Building right side up, 43
Building upside down, 9, 43
Butt joints, 11, 83
Buttock lines, 170
Buttstraps, 85

Cardboard, 60
Cartopper, 72, 75–102
Carvel planking, 108, 141–145
Catboat model, 57–72
Caulking seams, 21–22
Centerboard, 85–86, 95–96
Centerboard pendant, 95
Centerboard trunk, 85–86, 88
Centerline, 28, 171–172
Cheek pieces, 63
Chine boats, 1–102, 169–173
Chines, 19–21, 43, 47
Clamps, 127
Classic in Plywood, A (Payson), 52
Cleats, 98; thumb, 19
Clew, 99–100
Congdon, Albert, 107
Constant-speed drill, 126
Cradle, 102
Crosscut saw, 33
Cross-planking, 13
Crowning board, 135, 159

Decks, 2–6, 70, 159–160
Delta bandsaw, 138
Diagonals, 173
Dillion, Dave, 28, 147
Disc sander, 126

Dolly Varden, 122
Dory model, 27–54
Double-ender, 106
Drag strips, 22
Drawing board, 169
Drawknife, 35
Dremel Moto-tool, 119, 126, 137
Drills, 126
Duratite plastic wood dough, 37, 127

Edge set, 48, 60, 61, 77
Elmer's White Glue, xvii, 89
Enlarging plans, 169–173
Erismann, M.C., 147

False stem, 50
Farmer, Weston, 57, 60, 122
Fiberglass cloth, 38
Fiberglass mat, 39
Fiberglass model, 37–42
Fisherman's skiff model, 9–24
Fitting out, 90–91, 127–131
Flat-bottom boats, 171, 172–173
Floor platform, 90
Floor timbers, 130
Floquil's scale model paints, xviii
Foot stretchers, 51, 95–96
Forefoot, 136
Foresheets, 90–91
Formica model, 54
Forward perpendicular, *See* F.P.
F.P., 110
Framing, 85, 127–131, 136, 143, 145;
    two-part, 129
Franklin Titebond glue, xvii, 87, 89,
    120, 156
Friendship sloop model, 147–164

Garber, John, 75
Gelcoat, 41
Glossary, 175–179
Gloucester Light dory model, 27–54,
    167
Glues, xvii, 29, 85–86, 87, 89, 109, 120,
    155, 156; removing, 22, 126, 130, 131
Gluing, 29, 67, 85–86, 87, 89, 117–118,
    120–121, 126–127
Grids, 170
Gronros, Axel, 1, 9
Gudgeons, 93
Gunwales, 23, 51, 91–92, 126–127,
    134–135
Gypsy, 75

Half-breadth view. *See* Plan view
Half model, 42
Hamilton's Marine, 174
Handsaw, 3
Hand tools, xvi–xvii
Hanna, Jay, 117
Hardware, 93, 94, 100–101, 136–139,
    174
Hawse holes, 36–37
Hollow lifts, 156
Hull assembly, 29–35, 41–42, 87–89,
    134–136, 157–158, 161–164

Instant Boats, 59
Interiors. *See* Fitting out

Jigs, 9–11, 44, 156

Keeping the Cutting Edge (Payson), xv
King plank, 70
Kite string, 100
Kits, 174
Knees, 136

Leech, 100
Leg-o'-mutton rig, 98
Lift method, 148, 155-165
Limber holes, 62, 85
Little Hattie, 147, 148
Load waterline. *See* LWL
Lobsterboat model, 1–6
Lofting, 28, 169
Luff, 99
LWL, 97

Maine lobsterboat model, 1–6
Mansir, Richard, 144
Mantelpiece model, 69–72
Marking gauge, 119
Mast partner, 91
Mast rake, 62–63
Masts, 70–72, 98–102
Mast step, 90
Materials, xvii–xviii, 60, 84, 155–156,
    174. *See also* Wood
McInnis, Eldredge, 165
Measurements, xviii. *See also* Scale
    rule
Metalsmithing, 93, 137–139
Micro-Mark, xvii–xviii, 138, 174
Model-aircraft plywood, 60, 84
Modelbuilding, 167–168
*Modeler's Guide to Hull Construction,
    A* (Mansir), 144
Models: bread-and-butter, 147–165;
    fiberglass, 37–42; formica, 54; half,
    42; mantelpiece, 69–72; planked,
    9–24, 43–52, 57–72, 75–102,
    105–145; solid, 1–6, 28–37
Mold layup, 38–40
Mold station lines, 33–34, 61–62,
    169–170
Mold stations, 28–29, 44, 109–117
Montgomery, Elmer, 106–108, 117, 136
Multi-chine boats, 171

National Fisherman, 57, 60
Newark Dressmaker Supply, xvi, 174
Newbert and Wallace Shipyard, 107,
    164
Nylon kite string, 100

Oarlocks, 136–139
Oars, 136, 139–140

Paint brushes, xviii
Paints, xviii
Pauline, 148, 156, 164–165

Payson, David, 1
Payson & Co., H.H., 174
Payson's Patent Glue Spreader, 120–121
Peapod model, 105–145
Perpendiculars, 169; aft, 116; forward, 110
Pickup stick, 172
Pigtail, 98, 102
Pincurl clips, 120
Pinholes, 24
Pintles, 93
Planked models, 9–24, 43–52, 57–72, 75–102, 105–145
Planking: bottom, 21–22, 48–50, 77–83; carvel, 108, 141–145; cross, 13; strip, 120–127; tapered, 123–124; twisted, 124
Planks: king, 70; starter, 122, 124–125; whiskey, 67. See also Sheer strakes
Plans, xviii–xix, 174; Cartopper, 78–82; catboat, 64–66; dory, 30–31; enlarging, 169–173; lobsterboat, 4–5; peapod, 110–115; sardine carrier, 166; skiff, 14–17; sloop, 149–154
Plan view, 148, 171
Plugs, 28–29
Plywood, 60, 84
Polyester resin, 37–38
Power tools, xiv–xv
Profile view, 29, 34–35, 148, 170–171

Rabbet, 119
Rabl, Sam, 135
Removing glue, 22, 126, 130, 131
Resins, 37–38
Ribbands, 143, 145
Rigs: leg-o'-mutton, 98; spritsail, 98–102
Rocker, 33
Rockland Boat Shop, 1, 9
Rope eye, 100
Round-bottom boats, 105–165, 170–171
Rudder, 69–70, 92–93

Sabersaw, 3
Sails, 98–102

Sanding, 22, 35–36, 126
Sanding batten, 155, 162
Sanding block, 21
Sardine carrier model, 164–165
Saw blades, 12, 138; skip-tooth, 2, 32
Saws, 3, 155; band, xv, 3, 138, 155; bow, 3; crosscut, 33; hand, 3; saber, 3; scroll, xv, 155; table, xiv–xv, 2, 10, 12, 155
Scale rule, 18, 169
Scribing, 96–97
Scroll saw, xv, 155
Scull notch, 51
Sea Hawk, 54
Seams, 21–22
Seat risers, 23, 131
Seats, 23–24, 49, 131; bow, 90–91
Seizing, 101
Shaw & Tenney oars, 139, 140
Sheer batten, 46, 48
Sheer lines, 32–33, 46–47, 158–159, 160, 170–171
Sheer strakes, 122–123, 143
Sheet hooks, 95–96
Shutter. See Starter plank
Sides, 19–21, 48–50
Skeg, 36, 38, 39–40, 41, 51, 69, 92–93
Skiff model, 9–24
Skip-tooth blade, 2, 32
Sling, 98, 100
Sloop model, 147–164
Small Boat Journal, 57
Snotter, 98, 100
Snow's Shipyard, 107
Soaking wood Eskimo style, 127
Solid lifts, 156
Solid models, 1–6, 28–37
Spectre, Peter, 147, 167
Spiling, 46–48, 121
Spray adhesives. See Glues
Spritsail rig, 98–102
Staining wood, 91, 126
Starter plank, 122, 124–125
Stations. See Mold stations
Stem cap, 21, 50–51, 91–92
Stemhead, 136
Stems, 36, 44–46, 83–85, 88–89, 117, 136, 171; false, 50
Sternpost, 117, 136

Story pole, See Pickup stick
Strip planking, 120–127
Strongback, 60
Superglue, 85–86, 156
Suppliers, xvii–xviii, 174

Table saw, xiv–xv, 2, 10, 12, 155
Tack, 100
Tapered planking, 123–124
Templates, 29, 44, 48, 59, 60–61, 77, 155, 156
Thimble, 100
3M Spra-ment, 109
Thumb cleat, 19
Tiller, 70, 94–96
Tombstone, 32, 44–46
Tools, xiv–xvii, 3, 35, 119, 126, 137, 155–156, 169, 174; hand, xvi–xvii; power, xiv–xv
Transom, 77–83. See also Tombstone
12-foot fisherman's skiff model, 9–24
Two-part framing, 129

Ullom Co., R., 174
Understanding Boat Design (Brewer), 94

Variable-speed drill, 126
Varnishing, xviii, 24, 126
V-bottom boats, 171, 173

Wale, 143. See also Sheer strakes
Waterline, 96–97, 170; load, 97
Waxes, 38
Weldwood dry powder glue, 29, 156
Whiskey plank, 67
Whitmore, Alton, 129
Wilcox-Crittenden oarlocks, 137
William Underwood, 165
Wingnut, 93
Wood, xiii–xiv, 59–60, 91, 155; soaking, 127; staining, 91, 126
WoodenBoat magazine, 124, 147, 148, 174
Wood grain, 10, 35, 84, 118, 120, 133
Wood knots, 29, 36–37
Working craft, 168